TIMELESS TEACHINGS

BY

NORVEL HAYES

HARRISON HOUSE
Tulsa, Oklahoma

All Scripture quotations are taken from the *King James Version* of the Bible.

18 17 16 15   10 9 8 7 6 5 4 3 2 1

Timeless Teachings
ISBN-13: 978-160683-168-7
Copyright © 2015 by Norvel Hayes
P.O. Box 1379
Cleveland, TN 37311

The Blessing of Obedience, Copyright © 1982 by Norvel Hayes
ISBN-13: 978-0-89274-355-1

Confession Brings Possession, Copyright © 1993 by Norvel Hayes
ISBN-13: 978- 0-89274-639-2

How to Get Your Prayers Answered, Copyright © 1981 by Norvel Hayes
ISBN-13: 978-0-89274-215-8

Number One Way To Fight The Devil, Copyright © 1978 by Norvel Hayes
ISBN-13: 978-0-89274-094-9

What To Do for Healing, Copyright © 1981 by Norvel Hayes
ISBN 13: 978-0-89274-216-5

Why You Should Speak in Tongues, Copyright ©1982 by Norvel Hayes
ISBN-13: 978-0-89274-244-8

Published by Harrison House Publishers
P. O. Box 35035
Tulsa, Oklahoma 74153

Contents

THE BLESSING OF OBEDIENCE

THE BLESSING OF OBEDIENCE

In those days came John the Baptist, preaching in the wilderness of Judaea, and saying, Repent ye: for the kingdom of heaven is at hand. For this is he that was spoken of by the prophet Esaias, saying, The Voice of one crying in the wilderness, Prepare ye the way of the Lord, make his paths straight.

And the same John had his raiment of camel's hair, and a leathern girdle about his loins; and his meat was locusts and wild honey.

Then went out to him Jerusalem, and all Judaea, and all the region round about Jordan, and were baptized of him in Jordan, confessing their sins.

But when he saw many of the Pharisees and Sadducees come to his baptism, he said unto them, O generation of vipers, who hath warned you to flee from the wrath to come? Bring forth therefore fruits meet for repentance.

Matthew 3:1-8

When was the last time you won a soul? When was the last time you gave something to a needy person?

When was the last time you took God's healing power to the sick?

Pause for a moment and ask yourself these questions. When was the last time you—not somebody else, but *you*—brought forth fruit to the Lord? If you're trying to live a Christian life without bringing fruit to Jesus, you are a rebellious child of God. You are cutting yourself off from the many blessings God has for you.

God likes busy men and busy women. An idle mind is the devil's workshop. If you'll worship God, read the Bible, pray in tongues, win souls, pray for the sick, and cast out devils, you'll never go crazy.

If you'll be willing to obey God, He will keep you so busy that demons can't catch you.

They won't have a chance to get into your mind. Devils can't get in your mind anyway unless you think about them. You have to first think about the temptations they offer you, and then begin to yield to them.

The Bible says that in order to work for God and not be rebellious, you have to keep your flesh under subjection. It is the nature of the flesh to rebel against the things of God.

Confusion Causes Rebellion

Until I was baptized in the Holy Ghost, I didn't fully understand some things.

I was raised in the Baptist Church, and we didn't believe in healing, casting out devils, speaking in tongues, or operating in the gifts of the Spirit. A person could get saved or born again there; but it was foolish to take a cancer patient to our church to get healed.

You may ask, "Why don't churches like that get people healed?" Because they haven't received the truth of Mark 11:24 and James 5:14; they are still doubting and wondering. As long as you are a rebel against a particular portion of the Bible, God won't work for you in that area.

My Baptist mother died of cancer at 37 years of age. My brother, a football player in high school, died at 19 of Bright's disease. Nobody ever told them that Jesus was a healer.

Most of the people we knew were ashamed of it. All of us boys in the First Baptist church were ashamed. We wouldn't have been caught dead in a tent meeting that said, "Healing Crusade." We didn't know that the preacher under the tent was perhaps the only one in town to have the truth.

There we were making five thousand dollars a week, wearing our tailor-made suits, riding in Cadillacs, and going to the First church, saying, "We've got it. Those other people are just wild. We ought to feel sorry for them."

To be truthful, we were more confused than the devil because even the devil knows Jesus will heal people. (It's awful to be more stupid than the devil!)

We were in rebellion against God and the Bible. If you want to know what God is like, read the Bible. Jesus said, **Lay hands on the sick, and they shall recover** (Mark 16:18).

God sent me to a Full Gospel church there in Cleveland, Tennessee, to train me; but I was so rebellious that I was ashamed to go inside. I would look both ways to see if any of the First Baptist boys were watching. I knew God wanted me there, but I didn't want any of my relatives and friends to see me going in.

Bring Fruits to God

We have to learn not to be rebellious against God. People could prevent much of this rebellion if they would learn to bring fruit to God.

Don't be concerned about what the other fellow is doing; be concerned first about what you are doing for God. You must reach the point that you are willing to put your own desires aside and do what God wants you to do. When you cross that line, God will bless you. You will be in the place for God to give you His peace 24 hours a day, 365 days a year.

I am never confused about anything. I haven't had a confused day in years. I have the peace of God in me all the time—24 hours a day, 365 days a year. I don't believe in sad days.

Now I didn't say that the devil doesn't try to visit me; but when he does, I just say, "In Jesus' name, go from me!" Then I begin to worship the Lord. I say, "Oh Jesus, I worship You and praise You." Every morning when I open my eyes, I say several times, "I love You, Jesus." Then I try to

10

spend some time just worshiping Him. When I do, His warm and tender presence just comes on me.

Next, I begin to confess who I am in Christ Jesus. I confess that I am not a rebel against God. I say, "The Bible says in 1 Samuel 15:23 that rebellion is the same as witchcraft. I am not a rebel against God." Then I confess that I will do what God wants me to do.

Some people say, "It's so hard to live the Christian life." But if you present yourself to God like this, you will find that it's the easiest thing you ever tried. Don't be a rebel against the Bible, God, Jesus, and the Holy Ghost. When the Holy Ghost tells you to do something, do it!

One time the Holy Ghost told me to park my car in front of a parsonage and start praying in tongues. I lay down in the front seat and began to cry and make intercession for the pastor's daughter, who was considering marrying the wrong person.

The Holy Ghost knows exactly what He is doing. After I had been there about an hour, praying in tongues, the Spirit of God suddenly came upon the daughter in the house and she began to scream. She ran outside and jumped in my car, shouting, "I don't want to give him up! I don't want to give him up! Do I have to give him up?"

I said, "Yes, you have to give him up." She replied, "But it's not easy to give up somebody like that."

Obedience Produces Fruit

Obeying the Holy Ghost, then, involves bringing forth fruits. John the Baptist said, **Bring forth therefore fruits meet for repentance: and think not to say within yourselves, We have Abraham to our father: for I say unto you, that God is able of these stones to raise up children unto Abraham** (Matt. 3:8,9).

The average person will say, "I'm okay; I belong to such-and-such church." A national survey says that over 95 percent of the Christians in America have never won a soul and that over 60 percent of the born-again Christians in our country learned the foundation of the new birth through a book or a tract.

No wonder God told me several years ago to sow seeds on college campuses by giving out books and tracts. I have given out books and tracts by the hundreds of thousands from the University of Maine to the University of California. At first I could hardly believe that God wanted me to do it; I was already so busy. But I didn't question it.

God spoke to me as I was sitting in a sorority house at the University of Florida. About 85 girls in the dining room began to sing a dirty song. (I was the only man in the house.) I dropped my head and began to pray. I said, "Help these girls, Jesus. Get to these students."

I had been praying for about five minutes when the Spirit of God came on me and said, "I will if *you* will; but I *can't* if you *don't!*" Jesus wanted to walk into that sorority house and save every girl, but He couldn't. The Gospel is spread through men. The Gospel is spread through you, and it won't get spread if *you* are a rebellious child.

Beware of rebellion against God! Not too long after that, I told God I would begin a campus ministry. I continued to tell Him that for about three months, but I never did anything about it. Then I was in Memphis holding a meeting for several hundred young people. Someone walked up to me and said, "God told me to give you a motor home."

Another person put a $100 bill in my pocket. Then three fraternity boys from Memphis State walked up and said, "While you were speaking, Jesus told us to start working for you, handing out tracts and books."

I thought, "Dear Lord! A man has given me a motor home; another fellow hands me a $100 bill to buy some tracts; and three boys come up and say, 'Here we are.'"

Then the Lord said to me, "Get it?" For the next three years I had four or five witnessing teams covering college campuses across the country. Finally, I said, "Well, I've covered the country four or five times now. I guess I can let this ministry drop off to the side."

At this time I was in Nashville with Reverend Kenneth Hagin and his wife, Oretha. As I was getting ready to go back home, they said, "Norvel, the Lord wants us to pray before you leave." The moment we began to pray, the Spirit of God hit Brother Hagin. He started to cry and say, "Precious, precious, precious is the ministry to the young people. Precious is the ministry to the college kids."

Needless to say, God got through to me; and I repented. *God* had never told me to stop; *I* had said I was going to stop. But God never wants you to stop until *He* says so.

Don't rebel against God. If He tells you to do something, go ahead, even if it looks so big you think you can't do it. You'll be able to if you start out slow and start out small. The Holy Ghost will help you.

Can God Trust You?

God only helps and promotes those He can trust. The Spirit of God will help you if He can trust you. If He has never helped you do anything, then He can't trust you.

The same is true with the gifts of the Spirit. The Holy Ghost will give you the gifts as you minister. They will flow through you as the Spirit wills if He can trust you with them.

Ask yourself right now, "Can Jesus trust me to worship Him and to bring forth fruit unto Him?"

It isn't enough to say, "I belong to the Methodist church or the Pentecostal church." You can't just say, "I've been a church member for twenty-five years." It isn't enough to join a nice church in your community, go there every Sunday, and get mad if you don't have a good, spiritual service.

When are you going to sow seed yourself? Have you ever brought a sinner to church? God wants you to win souls yourself. Sure, you need a spiritual church where you can learn to worship God and work; but God wants you to bring forth fruit unto Him, and you will never bring it forth as long as you are a rebel against God and His Word.

Be Delivered From Yourself

If you're not bringing forth good fruit to Jesus, you need to be delivered from yourself.

One time when I was asked to minister God's Word at a large university, I was given a meeting room for a week. In one of the meetings an alcoholic was delivered and later brought the university psychiatrist. The psychiatrist sat and listened; then after the service he said to me, "I want to make an appointment to talk with you when you are available."

I said, "Okay. We'll talk this afternoon." As we talked together, he said, "I've never before heard anybody like you, and I've never sat for three hours without smoking a cigarette. I guess you know that my mind is telling me what you're saying isn't true."

I said, "I know your mind is telling you that; but, Doctor, I can help you if you'll let me. Just pull that intellectual mind out of your head, lay it aside, and come to God as a little child. Say, 'God, I'm dumb; but I'm willing for You to teach me. Teach me Your ways, Lord. Show me Your reality.'"

Then the Holy Ghost began to show me something about him. I said, "All day you tell people how to live. Then you go to the country club every afternoon and sit with your friends, drinking and telling dirty jokes. How many times have you sat there after telling people how to live all day long and not even known how to live yourself? How often have you said, 'Is this all life has to offer?'"

"Oh, I've said that a lot of times. How did you know?"

"Doctor, God will give you a brand new life. You don't know anything about God—you're a rebel against Him—but if you'll let me, I'll teach you enough to find Him. Come to class tonight."

That night I spoke on "God's Double Dose." I talked about being baptized in the Holy Ghost, speaking in other tongues, and being healed. When I got through, I gave an invitation for healing. The moment I gave it, the psychiatrist jumped out of his seat, came down in front of the whole class, and stood there. He was ready to receive from God!

The first thing you must do in order to receive from God is to get delivered from yourself. Like the psychiatrist, you have to forget about the people around you and put your pride aside. You have to be delivered from yourself—not somebody else, *yourself*.

Use What God Gives You

Suppose a radio pastor suddenly said, "Well, God, I think I'm going to cancel about 450 radio stations and speak once every three months. I've got enough money to get a place in Florida, so I'm just going to take it easy for a while. But I love You, Lord!"

After about three months, the things God had blessed him with would begin to drop off. Why? Because he wasn't using them. You have to use what God gives you. If you don't, it will get stale.

Jesus gave us the Great Commission, and He expects us to use it. He said:

> And Go ye into all the world, and preach the gospel to every creature ...
>
> And these signs shall follow them that believe; In my name shall they cast out devils; they shall speak with new tongues;
>
> They shall take up serpents; and if they drink any deadly thing, it shall not hurt them; they shall lay hands on the sick, and they shall recover.
>
> Mark 16:15,17,18

Don't be rebellious against God. Do what He has told you to do. Cast out devils when you come upon them. (But don't look for a devil behind every tree; devils aren't in everybody.) When you come upon a sick person, lay your hands on him.

Recently while speaking in Atlanta, Georgia, I gave an invitation, and a man stumbled to the front. You could tell he was a wino; he was filthy and the smell was almost unbearable.

He looked up at me and said, "The church I went to threw me out three times; but something told me that if I came here tonight, you wouldn't throw me out."

I replied, "That's right. You won't get thrown out of here. Come here."

I put my arms around him, and the Spirit of the Lord began to come upon him.

You might ask, "How could you put your arms around someone so filthy and dirty?"

God has delivered me from tailor-made suits and Cadillacs. I still have some of these things, but I have been delivered from them. (It's all right to have things as long as you're delivered from them—as long as they don't have you!)

It was nothing for me to put my arms around that man and say, "We love you. Get on your knees right now, and we'll pray for you. It doesn't make any difference how many bottles of whiskey you've drunk, we'll get hold of God for you and you won't be drinking anymore. When God comes, the whiskey goes."

Today, that person doesn't even look the same. He goes to that church and wears clean clothes now.

Jesus has never turned against lonely, hopeless drunks, and He never will. But He has to work through you. God wants good fruit.

Ministering In The City Dump

Years ago, I got delivered from myself at the city dump. I had seen that God was going to use me and thought He had made a mistake. For three or four years, I tried to talk Him out of it. Every night He would come into my room.

I would get out of bed and cry, "God, You don't want me; I'm no good. I've never done anything for You. I'm not a preacher. You don't want me, Lord."

But He acted like He had no ears. He would say to me, "Come, follow Me, and believe the Bible."

When I saw that He wasn't going to give up, and that He loved me enough to come into my room every night, I made up my mind to follow Him and do what He wanted me to do.

I said, "God, I don't have any sense, so You'll have to train me." I thought He would send me to a church or to a big auditorium; instead He sent me to the city dump! The houses there were pitiful; the people who lived there were in bad shape. They smelled so bad that I had to hold my nose to pray for them.

I never will forget the time I prayed for a woman while bugs were crawling on the bed with her. It isn't nice to stand beside somebody's bed and try to pray while the bugs are crawling out!

After I finished praying for her, I walked across the street to a house that must have had 40,000 flies inside! A woman lived there with her three children.

A little girl walked over to me and said, "Mister, this is all the milk the baby has, and we don't have any food. We don't have anything."

I walked outside and said, "God, is this what I get for leaving my church?" It was a Bible course straight from heaven! When I said that, God overshadowed me and I broke down. I will never forget it as long as I live.

He said, "Son, be faithful to Me here and I'll promote you."

"Yes, Lord."

"They need some milk in the house. What are you going to do about it?"

"Well, Lord, I'm going to the store and buy some milk and food."

"Show Me. Talk is cheap."

God is always wanting you to show Him something. Until you start doing something, you are a rebel against God.

Again, I quote John the Baptist: **And now also the axe is laid unto the root of the trees: therefore every tree which bringeth not forth good fruit is hewn down, and cast into the fire** (Matt. 3:10). By showing God something, you are bringing forth good fruit.

My Will Vs. God's Will

Several years ago God taught me a lesson. I thought that when I became born-again and Spirit-filled, I could do whatever I wanted to do. I wasn't interested in bringing forth good fruit to God the way I should have been.

One weekend I made up my mind to drive from Cleveland, Tennessee, to Augusta, Georgia; stay there for two days visiting; leave Augusta Saturday morning; go to the University of Georgia campus; watch Tennessee beat Georgia; then drive home after the ball game.

That was how I planned to spend my weekend, and nothing was going to interfere with it.

While in Augusta, a Full Gospel pastor said to me, "Brother Norvel, the Lord told me He wants you to speak at my church Sunday morning." I didn't know what the Lord had told him because I hadn't listened to the Lord myself.

If you make plans without praying, you'll miss God every time. Don't do it. You'll be in rebellion against God. Once you make up your mind, God can't reach you.

God will let you do all kinds of things that you shouldn't do. If you don't go to him in prayer and learn to be led by the inward witness, you will end up making a lot of mistakes.

If you feel in your spirit that you shouldn't do something, then don't do it. If you feel good about it — like velvet on the inside — that's the signal from the Holy Ghost to go ahead. The Spirit of God is here to help you and He will — if you pray and let Him lead you.

I hadn't prayed about my plans for the weekend. I just said, "I'm going to the ball game Saturday. I've already made up my mind."

When the pastor invited me to speak, I made up an excuse and said, "I'll come back and speak for you some other time."

The pastor had said he wanted to see me; so Saturday morning on my way out of town I stopped by his house. He had gone to the church, and I was sitting in his living room with some other people. Suddenly I began to feel pain around my heart. Then the pastor telephoned to say that the church janitor had just had a heart attack. Immediately we went into prayer.

In a few minutes he called back to report that the janitor had died. He asked, "Would you go with me to tell his wife? They own a store in town."

"Yes, I'll go."

So we went to the store and talked with his wife. All this time I was still planning to go to the Tennessee/ Georgia game.

While I was standing there in that store, the Spirit of God hit me like a bolt of lightning. The Lord said, "Go to the church and pray." The assistant pastor was standing there, so I told him what the Lord had said.

As I entered the church and was walking toward the pulpit, the Holy Spirit moved on me and I fell to my knees in prayer. I didn't know it, but the Spirit of God was making intercession for me. *For me!*

After I had prayed for about twenty minutes in the Spirit (in tongues), the Holy Ghost began to groan through me. I was lying flat on the floor in front of the pulpit, groaning. The Spirit of God had taken me to the point that all I could do was groan. For nearly three hours I lay there groaning before God. I couldn't get up.

After that time (just when Tennessee was beating Georgia!), I pushed myself up to a sitting position and said, 'All right, Lord, I'll speak at this church Sunday morning."

The Baptism of Fire

John the Baptist said:

> I indeed baptize you with water unto repentance; but he that cometh after me is mightier than I, whose shoes I am not worthy to bear; he shall baptize you with the Holy Ghost, and with fire.
>
> Matthew 3:11

There are three baptisms: water, the Holy Ghost, and fire. Nearly everyone believes in water baptism; many have experienced Holy Ghost baptism; but only a small number have been baptized in the fire of God.

As long as you leave off the fire, you will stay in some degree of rebellion as a child of God. But if you will spend time praying in the Spirit and yield yourself to Him—to the Greater One Who lives inside you—He will burn *you* out of you. (So many people want to do what *they* want to do, the way *they* want to do it.)

At that point in my life, I needed to be baptized in fire. I stayed in Augusta and spoke Sunday morning. The altar call lasted more than an hour. Fifteen or twenty people were baptized in the Holy Ghost, and many were saved. They flooded the altar.

Finally, we went to lunch about two o'clock. Again, I was planning to leave. As we were sitting there, I said, "As soon as we finish eating, I'm going back to get my clothes because I'm going home this afternoon."

But the pastor replied, "Oh, no, you're not! I'm going to get a revival out of this."

"A revival! No, pastor, be quiet!" He repeated, "I'm going to get a revival out of this. You're not going anywhere!"

But I insisted, "I am going home. I want to go this afternoon."

After that, I seemed to get weaker with every bit of food. I had to be helped into the car and into the parsonage. I went to sleep and woke up at 5:30, feeling refreshed; in fact, I felt like a teenager! I was ready to go; but by then it was too late to go home, so I decided, "I might as well stay and speak again tonight."

Burning Out the Chaff

What happened to me that weekend? In Matthew 3:12 John the Baptist is describing Jesus, the coming Messiah. He says:

> Whose fan is in his hand, and he will thoroughly purge his floor, and gather his wheat into the garner; but he will burn up the chaff with unquenchable fire.

God was burning the chaff out of me. The fire of God was burning *Norvel Hayes* out of Norvel Hayes. He was burning out that overwhelming desire for football games. (I still like football, but I'm usually too busy to go to games.) There is nothing wrong with football as long as you don't put it before God. I'm warning you: unless you want to wind up on the floor, groaning for three hours, don't put football games before God! He is no respecter of persons, and I've already been there, so take my advice.

Prayer Is the Key

Jesus was a Man of prayer. He would spend hour after hour in prayer before the Father God.

One year when I was a speaker at the Full Gospel Business Men's convention in Jerusalem, I stood in the Garden of Gethsemane where Jesus prayed until His sweat turned to blood. As I was standing there, His presence came upon me; it was a sweet experience!

Take my word for it, there is power in prayer. It makes you feel good to know that if you stay before God, you'll get some answers.

You can't defeat a person who prays. The storms may come, but he will just keep on praying until he prays himself out of them. He says:

"In Jesus' name, I will not take a storm from the devil. I belong to Jesus. I will not be rebellious; I will pray myself out of the storm."

Above all, you need to pray in tongues. To know the will of God, you need to pray in the Spirit continually. As you do, you will be walking in God's power.

The Bible says God's power is a way of life. That doesn't mean to worship God on Sunday, then go your own way on Monday, Tuesday, Wednesday, Thursday, Friday and Saturday.

If you are not spending time in prayer and worship before God, you need to be delivered from yourself. Until you are delivered from yourself, you won't bring forth good fruit.

Ask God in prayer to deliver you from yourself. As you begin to yield to the direction of the Holy Ghost, that element of rebellion will be removed from your life. The Lord Jesus Christ will be pleased with you, and God's power will become a way of living.

Confession
Brings
Possession

1

SPEAKING THINGS
INTO EXISTENCE

The Lord gave me insight on the subject of how Christians should talk. He never gives truths all at once because we can't take it. So He began teaching me on this subject nearly twenty years ago. I had just come out of a denominational church, and I had no idea what He was talking about.

I knew God had called me to teach the Bible. But He shocked me when He revealed Himself to me one day, and instructed me, "Norvel, I want you to start teaching the church—my children—how to talk." I didn't know what He meant.

Seeing Heaven

I have received a glimpse of heaven twice. I haven't seen all of it, but God has given me a glimpse twice. I have seen

enough to know that most Christians will be astounded
when they get to heaven. At that moment the truth will
be undeniably apparent because the Bible means what it
says— all the promises are ours. God promises several
hundred things in the Bible. Just think: There are hundreds of promises that belong to us, and yet we stumble
around trying to get a small headache healed.

All the promises belong to the believing Christian.
Whether we receive them or not is our choice. We may
want the promises, but we have to come God's way to
get them.

There is no question that God wants to heal believ-
ers. This is one of the promises that belongs to us. Many
Christians believe that Jesus *could* heal them if He wanted
to. The great news is that He wants to. And He wants to
do it now! But the question is, how do we get our healing?
It has to do with what God taught me. It has to do with
learning how to talk.

Don't Talk About the Mountains

That day, as the Lord instructed me in this area, He said,
"I told My children in My Word **that whosoever shall say
unto this mountain, Be thou removed...** (Mark 11:23).
But My children don't obey that. They don't talk to the
mountain. They want *to* talk to Me *about* their mountains.
This is unscriptural."

God doesn't want to talk to us about our mountains.
He doesn't have anything to do with the mountains

anyway. God doesn't have anything to do with our diseases. He didn't put disease, or any other type of affliction, upon human beings. Christians must be aware that if anything comes to bring harm, it does not come from God. God does not put things on us to cause us harm. He is a loving and gracious God.

> Every good gift and every perfect gift is from above, and cometh down from the Father of lights, with whom is no variableness, neither shadow of turning.
>
> James 1:17

This verse in James explains that only good things come from God. Good things come down from heaven. Heaven is another world where God lives. Heaven is a world where there is no sickness, there is no blindness, there is no flu, there are no bad colds. Heaven is a world of perfection.

If heaven is a world of perfection, and we have been born again by the blood of Jesus, and by the Spirit of God, then our names are written in heaven. We are citizens of that heavenly world.

Heaven is another world. It is the only real world there is. All the other planets, all the other worlds came down out of heaven by the mouth of God. God spoke planets, stars, suns and moons into existence. God *speaks* things into existence. The whole universe came about because God spoke it into existence. If Christians are ever going to have anything, they will need to speak things into existence, or they will not have them.

We may have some things, but I am talking about big things—things such as healing and financial miracles. We have some things simply by the process of natural learning, because we are natural human beings living in a natural world. But we have a spirit living inside our natural bodies, which has been reborn by the Spirit of God. The Holy Spirit of God lives inside our natural bodies. He wants us to have His divine nature (2 Peter 1:4), and this includes learning to do things His way—the way He instructs in His Word.

"I want you to teach my children how to talk," God said to me. "They won't talk to the mountains. They want to talk to me about their mountains. I have said to them, **Whosoever shall say unto this mountain, Be thou removed ....**"

Whosoever means any person. Anyone can say, "Cancer! Hey, Cancer, I am talking to you. You can't kill me. I command you, in the name of Jesus, remove yourself from me, Cancer. Hey, Cancer! You must go!" You have to talk so the cancer can hear you.

I hear people say, "We prayed, we believed and he still died." *You* prayed? What about the person with cancer? Did he speak to his mountain?

Churches Enjoy What the Preacher Speaks

If you are in need of a physical miracle, if you are in a life and death situation, you need to go to a church where the pastor believes in healing.

Every preacher gets what comes out of his mouth, in the same way that God gets what comes out of His mouth. Every church, every congregation, enjoys everything that comes out of the pastor's mouth. You may need to check up on your pastor. What he preaches is most likely what you are going to get from God, because most people who go to church believe what their pastor says.

If you have a bad liver, and your pastor believes that God will heal "some people some of the time," then you might as well find another church. If you don't, you will die. If your preacher preaches that God heals "some of the people some of the time," then the devil will always tell you that you just happen to be the one who is not in His will to heal. You cannot leave loopholes for the devil to add "if's" and "but's" and "maybe's." Believing in God's Word means that there is no more wondering because you either believe it, or you don't believe it. There is no in between.

❦

2

FIRST THINGS FIRST

Once a person accepts Jesus and repents, the Holy Spirit comes in to abide with that person forever. The Lord will never leave you nor forsake you. (Heb. 13:5.) What He wants to do is sup with you, and you with Him all the time. (Rev. 3:20.) God's number one motivation is not to make you rich, not to heal your body, not to give you a miracle. God's number one consuming fire and desire within Him is to have a relationship with each of His children. God wants you to repent of your sins and to accept His Son, Jesus, as your personal savior so you can dwell together forever.

If any cancer patient or lupus patient will kneel down—not because they have to be coached or told to, but on their own—and freely worship God, they will not die of that disease. But many churches are not teaching Christians how to worship the Lord. I went to church all my life, and no one ever taught me to worship God.

The three Hebrew children were delivered from the fiery furnace because they refused to bow their knee to a false god. (Dan. 3.) And if you will just worship God each morning without asking the Lord any- thing, He will deliver you. Worship Him first.

Understand that Jesus is not simply a "give me" Jesus. It is true that the Lord will **supply all your needs according to his riches in glory by Christ Jesus** (Phil. 4:19). But He is not just a "give me" Jesus. He is a God Who wants to be worshipped first of all. Christians need to learn to put first things first. Return to your first love (Rev. 2:4), and learn to worship Him.

It is very simple to learn to worship the Lord. Kneel down and tell Him you love Him. Or tell Him while you are lying in your bed before you arise each morning, or when you are taking a shower. Just lift your hands and worship Him. Do you ask Him for anything? No. Just worship Him. You can ask for things after you worship Him.

My ministry is involved in programs that feed people. I believe in feeding programs. In fact, I believe feeding programs should begin at home, in our nation. I am not too keen on feeding program ministries that are set up to feed people in another nation while people in their own home town are starving to death. We need to be faithful to those in our own hometown—to reach out to those who have no one to help them.

I was praying one day about our feeding program and the Lord said to me, "Not one human being since Adam was created—not one—has ever starved to death while they were worshipping and serving me. When the people bowed down and worshipped me, the rains came, and the fruit came and the grain fields flourished. The curse was lifted off their ground."

If the people of Ethiopia, where thousands and thousands of people have starved to death, would turn their hearts to God, He would bless their land. Years ago, they loved the Lord. Years ago, the people of Ethiopia would walk all the way to Jerusalem to worship God. The heart of God goes out to a people who will sacrifice to worship Him.

In the book of Acts, chapter 8, an angel spoke to Philip and directed him to go to Gaza in the desert. And there, riding in a chariot, was an eunuch who served under Candace, the queen of Ethiopia. As he was traveling along, he was reading the Scriptures out of the book of Isaiah. The Bible says this eunuch had come to Jerusalem to worship. Although he didn't fully understand the Scripture, he knew enough to *worship* and read the Bible. He knew that was the right thing to do.

When Philip asked the eunuch if he understood the Scriptures, the eunuch answered, "How can I, except some man should guide me?" So Philip climbed up into the chariot and explained fully to the eunuch about Jesus and the plan of salvation. The eunuch spoke with his mouth that he believed in Jesus Christ as the Son of God. The explanation was so clear that when they passed a body of

CONFESSION BRINGS POSSESSION

water, the eunuch was ready to be baptized. When they came out of the water, Philip disappeared. The Lord had translated him to another city. Both of these men obeyed God. It is amazing what God will do for those who obey and worship Him.

We can't go around trying to make God fit our approach to Him. We must study the Bible and learn how we can please the Lord. Ask yourself, "What can I do to please the Lord Jesus Christ?" You belong to Jesus now, you don't belong to the devil any longer, so study the Bible to see what you can do to please Him.

You will find out first of all that you can please Him by worshipping Him. You can learn that from the Ten Commandments. (Ex. 20.) The Word tells us we are to love Him with all our heart, mind, soul and strength. (Mark 12:30.)

Learning To Be a Giver

The next thing you will find that pleases God is for a Christian to be a giver—**loving thy neighbor as thyself.** (Mark 12:31.) Jesus explained that the second commandment is as important as the first.

A few years ago, God spoke to a man named Jack to pay his own expenses and travel with my ministry for six weeks. He was to sit on the front row every service, and watch the Holy Spirit at work. He did that. He came and traveled with me, sat on the front row and listened to every word. He began to get the truth down on the inside of him. Jack wasn't hesitant to give of his time and his money to learn about the workings of the Holy Spirit.

Jack's ministry was in Cleveland, Tennessee, for about three years. He spent hours and hours ministering to the down and out, the downtrodden of society. I saw him help set people free through God's Word. I called it "God's Spiritual Hospital." Fourteen of those whom he helped, enrolled in our Bible College. Fourteen in one year.

These were beaten-down people who had no one else to help them. They needed to receive intense training.

I respect Jack's ministry. It takes a special kind of love, a special kind of giving to minister to the outcasts of society. I respect Jack because he took the time, week after week, to teach and train people no one else cared about.

Yes, helping the downtrodden people requires more than prayer.

People must receive training intense training—to learn to walk in the fullness of life that God called them to. That training calls for undivided attention, because the devil will use every trick in the book to grab a person's attention away from the Word of God.

Holly, who sings at my services, has been listening to me preach every day since she was born. You can tell she has the Word in her. I didn't give it to her. She has received it and it is down on the inside of her. After she sings, she sits right on the front row. And she does this all the time. This is why God can use her. She is anointed and called of God. She is a giver. She is willing to give of herself.

Holly can sing one simple song and the Holy Spirit begins to work in the congregation. Two years ago when we were in Honolulu, I spoke in a small church of about twenty-three people. I gave the invitation and one woman came forward. I started to pray for her and the Lord checked me. The Lord said to me, "Have Holly come and minister a song to her."

I told her, "The Holy Ghost wants you to come here and sing a song to this woman."

Anytime I ask her to do something like this, she never questions, she never hesitates. She never says a word, she just does it. She began to sing, and I watched as the Holy Spirit came over the woman and ministered to her. She was healed as she stood right there, and she sobbed and sobbed. Then the blessings she was receiving began to flow into the congregation, and touched everyone there. All because a young girl was willing to give of herself and her talents.

It is imperative that Christians learn what pleases the Father. Two areas where we can begin to please God is in our worship and in our giving.

3

ALL THE PROMISES ARE OURS

...there hath not failed one word of all his good
promise, which he promised by the hand of Moses
his servant.

1 Kings 8:56b

For all the promises of God in him [Jesus] are yea,
and in him Amen, unto the glory of God by us.

2 Corinthians 1:20

If you will open your mouth and claim your rights in
Christ Jesus, you will live the abundant life. One afternoon
when I was holding a meeting in Cleveland, Tennessee, I
was in my room reading and the Lord spoke this to me,
"All the promises of mine are yours. Tell the Church, Son.
All the promises."

I said, "How can I get that across to them Lord? I am
trying to get them to believe for a little healing. And here
You are saying 'all the promises are ours'."

So why don't we have them? If God says all the promises are ours, why don't Christians have all the promises? Because we have to take them away from the devil. If you don't have enough joy in your life, you have to take it away from the devil. The Holy Ghost has joy. He can lay you out on the floor and make you laugh, and fill you full of His Joy.

> These things have I spoken unto you, that my joy might remain in you, and that your joy might be full.
>
> John 15:11

We Can't Judge God

> And all things, whatsoever ye shall ask in prayer, believing, ye shall receive.
>
> Matthew 21:22

This little verse will destroy most church doctrine. Does the Lord really mean we can have *all things* we ask for in prayer? "But Norvel, I know someone who believed and believed, and didn't get it."

There is no such thing as believing for something and not receiving it from God. There never was. If you believe it is possible to believe and not receive, then you don't understand the Scripture in the first place. You have been fooled along with everyone else who fails to receive what they ask from God.

41

People say, "We prayed, we believed and the Lord didn't do it." No human being in creation has ever believed God for something and didn't get it.

You can't judge God, and you can't judge the Word by what happened to someone you know. We are not smart enough to judge God. When God says it, simply believe it. God said if you believe it, you will receive it.

If you want to be healed, the Lord has healing power. That is one of His promises. His healing power is yours. The Lord wants to keep that healing power surging through your body by what you say.

What should you do if you have been prayed for to be healed? You should say, "Thank You, Jesus, for healing me. I just want to confess that You are my own personal Healer and I know You are healing me now."

When you confess that the Lord is healing you now—He is! If you don't say He is healing you now—He isn't.

You can get the healing power flowing through your body for a short period of time if the anointing comes on someone and it flows into you. But even after that, you must say, "Thank You, Lord, for healing me. Thank You that Your healing power is flowing throughout my whole body, in Jesus' name."

The key is to continually say these things with your mouth. Continue to speak into existence what you need.

4

SPEAK TO THE MOUNTAIN

When the Lord told me to teach His people how to talk, I didn't know myself what He meant. I said, "What do you mean, 'Teach your people how to talk'?"

He said, "Did you ever hear anyone hold a conversation with the flu?"

I said, "No, Lord. I never heard anyone hold a conversation with the flu. I never heard anyone hold a conversation with cancer. I never heard anyone hold a conversation with a bad liver. I never heard anyone hold a conversation with their mountains."

The Lord told me that the things that are wrong with Christians are their mountains, whether it be diseases or afflictions of any kind. Perhaps you have been searching for your healing for a long time, wondering how you can get God to heal you. You can learn how to do it God's way. You can be healed by speaking to your mountains—by telling them to be removed.

It Isn't Working

A few years ago, I was teaching at a Full Gospel Business Men's Fellowship in Indianapolis, Indiana. I had taught an after- noon session for one of their conventions. When I finished with the teaching, I closed my Bible and walked out of the auditorium. I had just walked out of the ball-room and was going down the hall toward the lobby. I heard a woman behind me say, "Mr. Hayes, I don't believe what you teach."

I stopped and turned around. There stood a neatly dressed, middle-aged lady. I answered, "Oh, really?"

"I don't believe what you teach," she repeated, "because it isn't true."

"I tell you what, my sister," I said to her. "Let's make a deal. If you will tell me what I taught this afternoon that wasn't in the Bible, first of all, I will apologize to God. Then, tomorrow afternoon, I will apologize to the entire convention when I teach. I will tell everyone there that I am very sorry. Then I will apologize to you and tell you that I am sorry. Because God called me to teach the Bible and that is what I do." Then I asked her to tell me what part of the teaching I had given that afternoon was not in the Bible.

She stammered a moment, and said, "I don't know."

I said, "You don't know? You have stopped me and made this bold statement and now you don't know?"

She answered, "Well, what I mean is, the things you teach don't work."

I responded, "So, now you are saying you are not sure whether or not it is from the Bible, but you are saying it doesn't work. If that is so, then you are saying the Bible doesn't work."

This seemed to upset her even more. Finally, she was able to explain why she was saying these things to me. It was because her husband had died at the age of forty-one from cancer. She said, "We prayed, and many other people prayed. We all believed for him to receive his healing, and he even believed the Lord was going to heal him. Right up until the moment he took his last breath, he believed God for his healing, but he died."

After a pause, she looked at me and added, "That's the reason I don't believe what you preach."

Flag Her Down

As she said that, the Lord spoke to my spirit and said, "Flag her down—she is on the wrong road. Flag her down with the truth from the Scriptures."

There are many Christians who have afflictions and diseases, or are buffeted with things God did not intend them to have. This does not mean they aren't good Christians. It simply means they are on the wrong road. They need to be flagged down and directed to the right road. If I can show them the *road of truth*, it will change their lives.

Notice the lady who stopped me after the meeting kept saying they believed the Lord was going to heal her husband. But the truth is, God is not going to heal anyone. So her belief was unscriptural. When your belief is unscriptural, then you don't get God's attention. You can pray and pray, but He won't do anything.

The Lord is not going to heal anyone. The Lord has already healed you. Jesus has the stripes on His back to prove He paid the price. It is up to every Christian to accept Jesus as the Healer. You must talk like He is your Healer, and talk like He is healing you now. That is the responsibility of every believer.

> Who his own self bare our sins in his own body on the tree, that we, being dead to sins, should live unto righteousness: by whose stripes ye were healed.
>
> 1 Peter 2:24

> But he was wounded for our transgressions, he was bruised for our iniquities: the chastisement of our peace was upon him; and with his stripes we are healed.
>
> Isaiah 53:5

A prayer that says, "I am trying to believe in a way that I can get God to make up His mind to have enough mercy to come in this room and heal this person," is unscriptural and will get no results.

The Lord instructed me to flag this lady down because she was on the wrong road. I asked her if she had her Bible with her. She did. I said, "Open your Bible to Mark 11:23." After she had located the Scripture, I said, "Now you believe Jesus, don't you?"

"Oh, yes, I love the Lord and I believe Jesus," she said. So I told her, "In this Scripture, Jesus is saying, **For verily I say unto you, That whosoever shall say unto this mountain, Be thou removed, and be thou cast into the sea ....**" Then I said, "See? There you are."

She shook her head. "See what? I don't see anything." She had not yet made the connection between this Scripture and her husband's untimely death.

So I took her back to the last four words of verse 22 where Jesus said, **Have faith in God.** Then I asked her, "Do you know what God is to you? God is the Bible. John 1:1 tells us **...the Word was God.** God was the Word, God is the Word and God will always be the Word forever and forever.

Psalm 107:20 tells us God sent His Word to heal. God gave us Jesus, and He gave us the Scriptures to heal us. When Jesus says to have faith in God, He also means for us to have faith in the Bible.

Personalizing the Scriptures

Even after pointing out these Scriptures to this lady, I could see she *still* didn't grasp the connection. I have learned through the years that I can teach and teach, but people will never receive permanent help unless I can get them to repeat back to me what I am teaching them. Even then, it may take days for them to comprehend the truth of the lesson. I knew this lady needed to say back to me what I was teaching her.

Finally, the Lord said to me, "Use his name, use the man's name." So I asked her, "What was your husband's name?" We will say here that it was John Smith. I asked her if she believed the Bible was written for every believer. She assured me she did. "If you believe that the Bible is for everyone, I would like to teach you how to personalize the Scriptures. I am going to read the verse again," I told her. "I will leave out some words and I will insert your husband's name instead, 'For verily I say unto John Smith, that John Smith shall say unto this cancer, be thou removed and be thou cast into the sea...'"

When I said her husband's name and the word cancer, I finally had her attention. She stepped back and looked at me with shock and surprise on her face.

"Mrs. Smith, let me ask you a question. Did you ever hear your husband talking to the cancer and saying 'Be thou removed'?" "No, sir," she said. Then she became calm. She had not been calm until that moment. She was an angry woman, and she was angry at me. Now in a soft, kind voice, she said, "No, Mr. Hayes, I never heard my husband talking to the cancer."

I said, "Do you see it? Do you see the truth in this Scripture?"

She said, "Yes, I see it." Then she added, "Do you mean we were only one Scripture away from my husband's healing?"

I answered, "I am not the judge of your husband. I am not the judge of anything. God didn't make me a judge.

48

God is the judge. God's Word doesn't need to be judged—the Word holds its own. The Word holds its own in the worst of circumstances on this earth. God's Word will speak loud and strong, with beauty and light, and with victory, under any circumstances if we have an unwavering faith. And we are asked to simply obey the words of the Lord Jesus Christ."

This dear widow began to weep. "Only one verse of Scripture and my precious husband could be living right now. Right now," she said.

Mrs. Smith was right. One verse of Scripture can save your home. One verse of Scripture can save your family. One verse of Scripture can save your life. Knowing God's Word is that important. The Bible has been given to us as a life saver. And Jesus is the life giver. After Mrs. Smith was able to regain her composure and speak again, she was one of the sweetest women I had ever met. She asked me to forgive her and I assured her that I did forgive her.

Again I said to her, "Do you see it?" She answered, "If my husband had done that, if he had obeyed Jesus, and obeyed the Word, he would still be living, wouldn't he?"

I said, "Yes, he would. Why wouldn't he? The cancer would have had to disappear. It could not have stayed."

Cursing the Roots

This is what Jesus explained to me about my daughter, Zona, when He took me in spirit to heaven and taught me about the growths on Zona's body. I had prayed for five years and the growths had not disappeared. The Lord taught me in heaven how to pray about this.

He said, "If you will curse the roots of those growths on your daughter's body, they will die and disappear. That is, if you believe and not doubt." He said, "Now, don't doubt Me, son. Don't doubt Me. If you curse them in My name, and talk to them and command them 'Get off my daughter's body'; if you believe and not doubt, they will disappear." Before I left, He reminded me, "Curse the roots of them, just like I cursed the roots of the fig tree." That's why I say Matthew 21:21,22 and Mark 11:23 are my favorite Scriptures. Jesus is truth and nothing but the truth. When Jesus tells me something, I believe it.

> And when he saw a fig tree in the way, he came to it, and found nothing thereon, but leaves only, and said unto it, Let no fruit grow on thee henceforward for ever. And presently the fig tree withered away.
>
> And when the disciples saw it, they marveled, saying, How soon is the fig tree withered away!
>
> Jesus answered and said unto them, Verily I say unto you, If ye have faith, and doubt not, ye shall not only do this which is done to the fig tree, but also if ye shall say unto this mountain, Be thou removed, and be thou cast into the sea; it shall be done.
>
> And all things, whatsoever ye shall ask in prayer, believing, ye shall receive.
>
> Matthew 21:19-22

> For verily I say unto you, That whosoever shall say unto this mountain, Be thou removed, and be thou cast into the sea; and shall not doubt in his heart, but shall believe that those things which he saith shall come to pass; he shall have whatsoever he saith.
>
> Mark 11:23

These Scriptures tell me I must *say* it. I must believe, but I must also *say* it.

Name It and Claim It

There are several evangelists going around the country now who are saying, "There they are: There's the 'Name It and Claim It' bunch." Personally, I would like to be the president of the "Name It and Claim It" bunch. I cast my name into the ballot box for president. I am pleased to be a member of the "Name It and Claim It" bunch.

I can prove by the Scriptures that if you don't name it, and you don't claim it, you won't receive it. And when people make light of that truth, it disturbs me.

Just because a preacher can preach a good sermon doesn't mean that a Christian should believe everything the preacher says. Just because an evangelist dresses nice and looks good doesn't mean he is preaching truth. If he makes fun of the Bible and Bible truths, you will have to pay for it. It is vital for a Christian to read the Bible and find out the truth for himself.

My admonition is that we be as smart as the old cow that has sense enough to eat the hay and leave the sticks.

There are no perfect preachers. There is no perfect human except Jesus. If the preacher says something that is contrary to God's Word, just disregard it. Accept the good things he says, but if he makes light of Scriptures, which he may not understand, don't accept what he is saying. You can learn to eat the hay and leave the sticks.

So when I hear reports of people making fun of us as the "Name It and Claim It" bunch, I ignore them. And I go on obeying God's Word and speaking to the mountains and cursing the roots.

Take Inventory of Your Body

If you will say to this cancer, "Hey, Cancer, I am talking to you. Remove yourself from my body, in Jesus' name. You can't live in me. You can't kill me. You can't even stay in my body. Go into the depths of the sea, in Jesus' name!" And if you believe and doubt not, the Lord said it shall be done! Do this every day.

Of course, this doesn't just mean cancer. You can take inventory of your body. Some people may have a long list of things that are wrong with them. Take that list and make several copies. Put one in every room in the house. Several times a day speak to those afflictions and command them to be removed from your body.

After you speak to the afflictions, then thank the Lord. "Thank You, Lord, for removing the infections from my blood system. Thank You that my blood is normal in Jesus' name."

Anything that is wrong with you can be your mountain, and you must learn to speak to it. It may be that your pocketbook is empty. If there are areas in your life that are not within the abundant life that Jesus promised (John 10:10), you need to apply this teaching to that area, and do something about it.

Blessings Are Not Automatic

The blessings of God will not come upon you automatically. If you are waiting for a financial blessing, or waiting for a physical healing, you will be waiting a very long time.

Why don't you talk to the devil concerning your money if you are broke? Say, "Devil, I am supposed to be living the abundant life. Satan, I take authority over you. Jesus says I can bind you, therefore I am binding you up so you cannot come against my money. I command you to turn my money loose, in Jesus' name."

Next, you speak to the money God has for you. God has a certain portion of financial blessing for you. Why don't you speak to it so it will come into existence?

"I command my money to come in to me, enough to pay all my bills, and thousands and thousands of dollars left over to spread the gospel and to buy what my family needs."

Some people will only say "hundreds" of dollars, but some people won't say anything at all. Why is this, when God has help for you?

...Let the Lord be magnified, which hath pleasure
in the prosperity of his servant.

Psalm 35:27b

For ye know the grace of our Lord Jesus Christ, that,
though he was rich, yet for your sakes he became
poor, that ye through his poverty might be rich.

2 Corinthians 8:9

These Scriptures clearly show that it isn't God's will
for His people to be poverty-stricken.

God intends for us to use this principle in all areas of
our life. You can speak to confusion to go. "Spirit of confusion, go from me. You cannot live in my mind. Confusion,
you must go from me. I command you to be removed, in
Jesus' name. I am talking to you, spirit of confusion."

Confusion is not of God. First Corinthians 14:33 says,
For God is not the author of confusion, but peace ...

It doesn't matter what the mountain is, if it is outside the abundant life that Jesus has designed for you,
command it to go. You have no business putting up with
it. The few Scriptures that I have mentioned here can
come against all the works of hell. Two or three Scriptures will work. You don't need to memorize the whole
Bible. Just learn to speak to the mountain. Talk to it and
watch it disappear. It's something you must learn to do
for yourself.

Do It Yourself

Because I have been speaking to mountains for years, people want me to speak to their mountains for them. "You know how, Norvel. Please speak to my mountain for me," they say. But anything I can do, you can do! Each Christian can learn to speak to the mountains.

The Scripture says, **...if ye have faith, and doubt not, ye shall,** [*you* shall, *you* shall!].... Not *me* doing it for you. Not anyone else doing it for you. If *you* speak to your mountain, it will be removed. The Lord will stand by His Word for you, as well as He will for me. Start speaking today as the Lord would have you speak—as the *child of a King* that you are.

Conclusion

God wants His children to learn how to talk: to learn to speak to mountains in their lives and tell them to be removed, to curse the roots of diseases so they will die, to speak things into existence just as God does. Once Christians learn how to talk, they will have the victory and will live the abundant life that God has promised.

How to Get Your Prayers Answered

HOW TO GET YOUR PRAYERS ANSWERED

Have you ever wondered why your prayers aren't answered even though you have prayed for months, or sometimes years?

I used to wonder about this myself. I would say, "I don't understand You, Jesus. Why don't You answer my prayer? I've got to have this, but it's not coming to pass. Why don't You answer my prayer?"

One day as I was reading the Bible, the Lord began to bring this message into focus. He began to unfold it right before me. Today I can see it so plain — just as if it had always been a part of me.

How To Approach God

The Lord is so good to us. He gives us different ways to approach Him and different ways to receive things from Him.

What I am going to share with you here is one of the most important truths in the Bible, and it's actually one of the easiest ways I know of to receive things from the Lord.

Many people won't go to God until the very foundation of their life has crumbled before them. Then because they have no place else to go, they go to God.

This is one of the best times for God to get hold of a person's life—when the circumstances of his life have crumbled and his heart is broken. God would like to get hold of us before that, but most people just won't go to God until they have to. They want to figure out everything for themselves.

If we will go to God with an open heart, ready to receive, He will be able to come into our lives and do what He wants to do with us.

The Bible says that God will reward those that diligently seek Him. (Heb.11:6.) You can't seek God just a little bit and expect to find all the "goodies" from heaven. They don't come that way. Your prayers will never be answered that way. You will have to diligently seek Him.

The most important thing is *how* you ask God for something—the kind of words you use when you speak to Him. When you pray, you are not talking to me, or to the pastor of your church, or to a friend—you are talking to Jesus.

He doesn't look at you from the outside, but from the inside. He doesn't hold your past sins against you. (The devil does, but Jesus doesn't.)

Be Sincere

Because He looks on the motives of your heart, you have to approach Him in the right way. You have to be sincere.

Jesus said, . . . **out of the abundance of the heart the mouth speaketh** (Matt. 12:34). When you start talking, Jesus will know right away the condition of your heart.

Many times, Jesus doesn't like the way we pray.

You may say, "But I'm humble when I pray. Sometimes when I pray, I even get on my knees and cry."

That doesn't make any difference. Jesus still won't answer your prayer if you pray wrong.

Hear and Understand

Let's look at the book of St. Matthew, chapter 15, beginning with the 10th verse:

> And he (Jesus) called the multitude, and said unto them, Hear, and understand:
>
> Not that which goeth into the mouth defileth a man; but that which cometh out of the mouth, this defileth a man.
>
> Then came his disciples, and said unto him, Knowest thou that the Pharisees were offended, after they heard this saying?

Many people are offended when they hear the Gospel straight from the pages of the New Testament. They are offended when you tell them what the New Testament says about speaking in tongues. They say, "We don't teach that in our church," but it doesn't make any difference what they teach in their church. It's what the Bible says that's the truth, not what anybody teaches in a church.

The disciples said, "You offended them, Jesus."

In verse 13, He answered them and said, **Every plant, which my heavenly Father hath not planted, shall be rooted up.** You can have all kinds of teaching in you, but unless God planted it there, it won't do you any good.

You might as well get rid of everything that's not in the New Testament—regardless of how many relatives you have who believe it that way. Just go ahead and read the New Testament for yourself. Believe what you read and act on it. You can receive it from Almighty God yourself.

It won't do you any good to go around and find out what everybody else believes. If you do, you'll hear 40,000 tales—and all of them will be different!

But God's Word won't change. It won't change because God doesn't change. Jesus stays the same all the time, and His Word stays the same. Every morning when you pick up the New Testament, it will be the same. It stays steadfast all the time, and it works all the time.

What does Jesus have to say about people who are offended by His Word? "Every plant that my heavenly Father has not planted will be rooted up."

Then in the 14th verse He says of the Pharisees, **Let them alone: they be blind leaders of the blind. And if the blind lead the blind, both shall fall into the ditch.**

Is that plain enough?

Jesus was saying to His disciples, "If they are offended at My sayings, let them alone. Stay away from them. They are blind. If you mess around with them, you'll be blind, too. You won't be able to see, and both of you will fall into the ditch."

Then answered Peter and said unto him, Declare unto us this parable (v. 15).

In other words, "Explain this parable, Jesus. Tell us what You mean."

And Jesus said, Are ye also yet without understanding? In other words, "What's the matter with you guys? You've been with Me for a long time—don't you understand yet?"

You know, I believe most of us are just like Peter. We are yet without understanding. I imagine if Jesus walked into a church service these days, He would probably say something like this: "You people are robbing yourselves. Are you yet without understanding of all the things in the New Testament that are for you? Are you yet without understanding of all the things I've told you in My Word?"

You could ask Him all kinds of questions, but He would always answer you with a scripture and say, "I've told you in My Word." It's not good enough for us just to be hearers of the Word. God wants us to be doers of the Word, not hearers only. (James 1:22.)

Speak the Word

In verses 17 and 18 Jesus says: **Do not ye yet understand, that whatsoever entereth in at the mouth goeth into the belly, and is cast out into the draught? But**

those things which proceed out of the mouth come forth from the heart.

What shape is *your* heart in? How have *you* been talking?

Have you been talking faith, or have you been talking doubt?

Have you been talking love, or have you been talking in a way that the love of God can't work?

> Those things, Jesus said, which proceed out of the mouth come forth from the heart; and they defile the man.
>
> For out of the heart proceed evil thoughts, murders, adulteries, fornications, thefts, false witness, blasphemies:
>
> These are the things which defile a man: but to eat with unwashen hands defileth not a man.
>
> Then Jesus went thence, and departed into the coasts of Tyre and Sidon (vv. 18-21).

It's not what you eat that defiles you, but what you say. It's what comes out your mouth that causes all the trouble in your life and discourages you from receiving from Almighty God.

Check Your Motives

Verse 22 says, **And, behold, a woman of Canaan came out of the same coasts, and cried unto him, saying, Have mercy on me, O Lord, thou Son of David; my daughter is grievously vexed with a devil.**

Her daughter was possessed by devils, so she approached Jesus for help.

Do you know what it's like to live in a house with someone who is possessed with devils? It isn't pleasant. I don't care how much you love that person from the natural standpoint, it still isn't pleasant. When you love Jesus and want to give your life to Him, it isn't pleasant to hear someone close to you curse God and act like the devil himself.

This woman who approached Jesus knew exactly what that was like. She cried out, "Have mercy on me, O Lord; my daughter is grievously vexed with a devil."

Verse 23 says, **But he answered her not a word**. Jesus wouldn't even talk to her.

Does that surprise you?

Don't you think that was a very humble way for her to approach the Lord? She came crying to Him, but He wouldn't even talk to her. He wouldn't pay any attention to her.

Why?

Because her motives were wrong. She was crying, "Have mercy on *me*, Lord," not, "Have mercy on my daughter."

Jesus looked on her heart as she cried, "Have mercy on *me*, Lord. I'm living in torment because my daughter is vexed with a devil."

Jesus didn't answer. He wouldn't even talk to her.

What does the Bible say He did?

He answered her not a word. In everyday language, that means He wasn't even talking to her. She was praying selfishly and Jesus wouldn't listen to her.

Let me ask you a question: Are you a parent with a wayward child—a child who doesn't know the Lord?

Here Jesus gives you the secret to getting your child back in tune with Him. Now if you don't do it, it won't be Jesus' fault. It won't be anybody's fault but yours.

You have probably spent many hours, praying for your child. When he first started going against your teachings, I'm sure you felt like all the blood had been drained out of your body. You probably felt like a failure. I know how you felt because I've been there. Sometimes you really feel sorry for yourself.

The only reason your child is wayward is because of the power of the devil. The only reason your child is like that is because the devil has tempted him and led him astray. It doesn't make any difference whether he is involved in drinking or dope or sex. In any case, the devil has taken over and caused your child to be separated from God.

You've prayed and cried and wept. You can't understand why God won't answer your prayers. Why won't He answer? Maybe your motive is wrong.

When you ask Jesus for something selfishly—if you have only yourself in mind when you pray—He won't give it to you.

Maybe you are living in torment. Maybe you are being buffeted by something and want to be released from it. When you pray, God looks inside you and sees your heart. It is no trouble for Him to look inside you; He made every part of you. He is interested in you, and He knows whether or not you are interested in making Him your God.

Spend Time With God

The number one thing God wants is to be your God and have you be His people. It would be so easy to receive things from God if you would open yourself to Him and let Him do what He wants in your life.

If you want to please the heart of God, place yourself before Him and let Him work His perfect will in your life. Just be like putty in His hands.

Sometimes you need to shut yourself off from "religious activities." Sometimes you need to shut yourself off from witnessing and teaching. Just go to God when no one else is around.

You shouldn't spend all your time going to meetings. You need to spend time loving and worshipping God, telling Him how much you love Him.

Don't allow yourself to get caught up in religious activities without putting Jesus first place in your life and worshipping Him when you are alone in your prayer closet. Don't let any work—I don't care what it is—take so much of your time that you aren't able to shut yourself off from it to worship Jesus. If you do, you'll cut yourself off from the blessings of Almighty God.

The more time you spend in your prayer closet, worshipping Jesus, the better warrior you'll be when you get outside.

Let God Be #1

So often we run around in our own religious Christian life, doing this and that at the church, trying to help people; but we don't spend any time alone with God. It's like we are partly lying to the people. We tell them how important Jesus is in our lives, yet He really isn't occupying that number one spot. Sometimes our God is religion and church, not Him.

God doesn't want your duty to be number one in your life. He wants to be number one. Don't push Him over to the side and do all the work for God without taking time to worship Him. If you do, you are lying—to yourself and to Him.

You can work for Jesus 15 hours a day, but if you don't take the time to spend even 15 or 20 minutes in private worship of Him, you are lying to yourself. He really isn't your number one God.

We are supposed to worship the Lord with all our hearts. Luke 10:27 says, **Thou shalt love the Lord thy God with all thy heart, and with all thy soul, and with all thy strength, and with all thy mind; and thy neighbour as thyself.**

Many times we miss God by getting our lives so involved in going to church and working for Jesus that we grieve His heart. I know we are going to be judged on the day of judgment by the works we do; but many people are trying to promote the Kingdom of God in the wrong way. They do it from an intellectual standpoint and from a labor standpoint. God is not pleased with that.

Let Him Love You

One day as I had just finished taping some radio broadcasts, the Spirit of the Lord came upon me in a sudden manifestation. During that time the Lord revealed to me what was wrong with the world. These were the words He said to me that day: "People make Me complicated. All I want them to do is let Me love them."

We don't let the Lord love us much. We're too busy. I get guilty of this myself. If you let the Lord love you, then His love can go from you out to others. You can have more understanding and more patience about things when you let the Lord love you.

Many people might think, "Well, the Lord loves me anyway."

That's not what He is talking about. If you would bow down to Him and worship Him in your prayer closet, then His power would come on you and melt your heart. He would begin to love you, and you would begin to love Him back.

All Jesus wants you to do is let Him love you. He wants to take you in His arms and love you. He wants to manifest Himself to you. He wants His pure love to flow down through your body and into your mind, just as if you had taken a bath.

If you don't spend any time before Him, it's hard for Him to get you still long enough to love you. He loves all of us in a general love, but that's not good enough. He wants to boldly show you how much He loves you.

His love will melt you down until you can have compassion on drunks and thieves and prostitutes. With His love in you, you can see people in a different light. You can see what sin and the devil have done to them.

If you will let God love you, you won't always just go to Him with the big mountain in your life.

If you have been praying for things and not getting any answers, start letting Jesus love you. Start worshipping Him and loving Him, telling Him how you feel about Him:

"Jesus, You're the Lord of my life. I thank You that You died on the cross for me. I worship You, Jesus, and praise You because my name is written in the Lamb's Book of Life. I worship You, Jesus. I praise Your wonderful name. I hold Your name above all names that are on this earth."

It's a good thing to be involved with a church and with God's work; but the greatest thing you will ever do is shut yourself off from the world and spend time with Jesus—just *you* and Him. Jesus wants *you*—just you alone. Spend time worshipping Him, and you will learn more about His beauty than you have ever known.

Worship Has Rewards

This woman in the 15th chapter of Matthew had to learn these things the hard way. Again, verse 23 says, **He answered her not a word. And his disciples came and besought him, saying, Send her away; for she crieth after us**.

But, of course, Jesus loved her. He knew she was in trouble. He didn't want to turn anybody away troubled, but she had to learn a lesson. You see, God has His own standards. We have to come His way; we can't come our way.

He answered His disciples and said, **I am not sent but unto the lost sheep of the house of Israel** (v. 24).

Now notice her second approach to Jesus in the 25th verse: **Then came she and worshipped him**. She said, "I worship You, Jesus. I love You."

As she was worshipping Him, she was saying, *Lord, help me.* She knew there was help in Jesus.

There was no worship involved in her first approach—when she cried out, "Lord, have mercy on me." That was a selfish prayer. She wanted to be relieved of the thing that was causing her so much trouble. She wanted to be relieved, but there was no worship in her plea. That's why Jesus wouldn't talk to her.

But when she came the second time, she was worshipping Him as her God, and He found favor in what she was doing. When God finds favor in the way you believe and talk and act, He will move for you.

When she came to Jesus the second time, He gave her a little test to see how sincere she was. He wanted the right words to come out of her mouth. He wanted her to talk right.

Verse 26 says, **He answered and said, It is not meet to take the children's bread, and to cast it to dogs**.

In other, words, He was telling her, "I'm a Jew, and I came for the children of the house of Israel. You're out of a different coast, from a different tribe. It's not right for Me to cast the children's bread to dogs."

Then verse 27 says, **And she said, Truth, Lord: yet the dogs eat of the crumbs which fall from their master's table**.

After she worships Him, she says, "Jesus, You are my Master, and I'm willing to eat even the crumbs that fall from my Master's table. I'm willing to take anything that you have to give me. I worship You, Jesus, because You are my Master."

Do you know what He did for her? Verse 28 says, **Then Jesus answered and said unto her, O woman, great is thy faith: be it unto thee even as thou wilt. And her daughter was made whole from that very hour**.

Jesus spoke the Word and it happened. The devil left her daughter, and she was made whole. Why? Because her mother pleased God.

Stand Steadfast In Faith

As a parent, you have spiritual authority over your child. It doesn't make any difference if your child rebels. I know because I went through this for a time with my daughter.

God dealt with me strongly about this one day. He said: "Son, I want you to understand something: There is no power on earth greater than My power—no power!

"Your daughter doesn't have the power and the faith to get out of the trouble she is in. It will have to be done by your faith in Me.

"I can set her completely free through your faith, but your faith concerning her has been wavering a little. You have started wondering about when I am going to do it. That is none of your business. I don't need your help. All I need is your faith. I have to have your faith before My power is even available to move on your child.

"Every time—not just part of the time, but every time—your faith wavers, it cuts off My power from dealing with her. You're her father, and your unwavering faith will bring My power out of heaven and upon her life to set her free.

"But your faith wavers from time to time concerning her complete freedom. Sometimes you even wonder if I am going to do it. When you waver, My power stops."

That's the reason Hebrews 11:6 says that without faith it is impossible to please God. You can't please God without faith. You *must* have faith. He wants you to recognize Him as your number one God. He wants you to know that He will work in your life. But to know that, you must spend time with Him and get to know Him.

If you will stand with an unwavering, steadfast faith, you can keep your child out of the hands of the devil. If your child is away from God now, you can bring him back to God.

If you will spend time worshipping the Lord through faith, the devil can't destroy your child. There is no way the devil can destroy any of your children if you will follow the Lord and listen to His instructions.

Confession Brings Possession

When I was holding a meeting in one church, a woman suddenly stood up in the audience and challenged me. I had been telling them that God would do anything for them if they would let Him.

She said, "Brother Norvel, you've been telling us for two or three days how much the Lord loves us and that God would do anything for us. What about our situation? My husband and I have a 17-year-old daughter that we love with all our hearts. About six months ago she just walked off from the house one day and never came back.

"Brother Norvel, I've prayed and prayed and prayed. Doesn't God know where she is?"

I said, "Absolutely."

"Will He show me where she is?" I said, "Sure, He'll show you where she is. "Well, as I've been sitting here listening to you, I'm beginning to see something I've never seen before. I feel like God requires something of me other than what I've been doing."

"Well," I said, "your faith can bring her in. You can speak her back into existence, back into your presence. I'll teach you how to do it if you want me to."

"I'll do anything you say," she answered. "Just tell me what to do, and I'll do it."

"Okay. Jesus said in Mark 11:23, **For verily I say unto you, That whosoever shall say unto this mountain, Be thou removed, and be thou cast into the sea; and shall not doubt in his heart, but shall believe that those things which he saith shall come to pass; he shall have whatsoever he saith**.

"Now, according to James 4:2,3, you have not because you ask not; and when you ask and receive not, it's because you ask amiss.

"I can imagine how the devil has treated you—how he has thrown darts of doubt into your mind about your daughter. He's probably told you over and over that she's been kidnapped and killed. He's probably told you all kinds of things."

She said, "Yes, he has. Sometimes I think she will call; then I'll begin to doubt and start thinking she's dead."

"Well, you can speak her back into your presence if you'll believe that those things which you say will come to pass. You can do it because this Scripture says you can— and it's the truth. God can't lie.

"I'll pray with you; then I want you to say this every day: 'Thank You, Jesus, for showing me where my

daughter is. Thank You, Jesus, for having her contact me.'
"Don't ever say anything else. Just keep it up every day. Keep firing down that same line. Then God will move on her heart. He'll have her get in touch with you. Your faith in His Word will cause her to do this. Her soul can be rescued through your faith."

She said, "Okay, I'll do it."

A few months later, I was back there ministering, and that same lady stood up and said:

"You know what you told me, Brother Norvel, that if my faith didn't waver, the Lord would move on my daughter? Sometimes I would do that day after day after day. The devil tried to tell me it wouldn't work, that it was too simple, that my daughter was dead. But I wouldn't listen to him.

"Every time I got to the point where I was about to doubt, the Lord would remind me of what you told me. Those words would ring in my head and I would say, 'No! I'm not going to doubt! I'm not going to doubt!'

"Then one day the phone rang, and it was my daughter on the phone! Not only that, but she was under conviction and crying. We drove over, picked her up, and brought her here to church. She gave her life to the Lord and Jesus baptized her in the Holy Ghost. She's sitting right over there."

When she told me that story, I was really blessed; but God added a bonus—a supernatural bonus. The Spirit of the Lord came on that young girl. She got out of her seat and walked very slowly up to me. She put her arms around my neck and just held on.

The Spirit of God was all over her. For about ten minutes, we just stood there together, weeping.

You know, all the money in the world can't buy that experience from me. It was glorious—an experience I will never forget.

Be A True Worshipper

Jesus said, **The hour cometh, and now is, when the true worshippers shall worship the Father in spirit and in truth: for the Father seeketh such to worship him. God is a Spirit; and they that worship him must worship him in spirit and in truth** (John 4:23,24).

If your prayers aren't getting answered, maybe you should check and see how much time you are spending before the Lord in worship and praise.

Set yourself to be a true worshipper. Put aside time for the Lord. Put Him first place in your life. If you do—I promise you—you will see your prayers answered.

THE NUMBER ONE
WAY TO FIGHT
THE DEVIL

THE NUMBER ONE WAY
TO FIGHT THE DEVIL

This message is one that God unfolded to me super-naturally and told me to teach to the Church.

You know by this time, that Jesus loves you and He causes you no harm. He comes to bless you. He comes to give you life and give it to you more abundantly.

All the bad things and the harm and the heartaches and things you've ever had in your life didn't come from God. They came from the devil. Now it is one thing to learn who Jesus is; it's another thing to learn who the devil is.

It's like this one family that said they had trained their children to know the Lord Jesus Christ all of their life. They're a good, sweet, precious Christian family. They received a phone call one night from the police station. The policeman said, "Is your name so and so?"

"Yes, it is."

"Well, this is the local police station and you better come down here. We're fixing to lock up your son (he was 17 years old), and he's going to be here a long, long time."

"Oh no, not our son. It couldn't be our son. Our son is a Christian. We've taught our son all about Jesus all his life. He's never caused us one minute's trouble. He knows the Lord Jesus Christ personally."

The policeman said, "I don't know about that ma'am. I'm just telling you, your son's down here and he told us to call you. He just shot somebody and tried to rape a girl and robbed a place all at one time. We've got about three big charges against him. He's going to be here a long, long time. You better come down here if you want to see him."

So the woman got all shook up and started wringing her hands, "Why God, oh why God? Why did this happen to us?"

That's what Christians usually always say: "Oh God, why did this happen to us?" God doesn't even have anything to do with it.

"Lord, why did this happen to us? We taught our son all about you Jesus, all of his life."

They went to the police station to talk to him. The mother was so shook up, they decided to call a Bible teacher for some words of comfort. So the Bible teacher got there and the lady began, "I don't know why this happened to us. We've taught our family all about Jesus. Oh God, why did this happen to us? Jesus why did this happen to us?"

"Wait a minute lady! Wait a minute! What do you mean talking this over with Jesus? You picked the wrong one."

"Ah, I have?"

82

"Yeah, that's right; you have. What are you blaming God for this for? God didn't have anything to do with this."

"Oh, but I've taught him all about Jesus all of his life."

"But Jesus doesn't make people rob places, rape girls and shoot people. Jesus is not guilty of that kind of junk. Let me ask you a question ma'am. Did you ever teach your son about the devil?"

She said, "No, I never did teach my son about the devil."

"Well this is a result of your teaching. Jesus is not guilty of making people do those things, the devil is. How would you like for the United States Army to draft your son at 18 years old and send him overseas in the battlefield with no basic training at all. He doesn't know how to dig a fox hole or even know to wear a helmet. How long do you think he'd last? Why, he'd get killed in 30 minutes. He wouldn't even know what to do."

The Devil is Crazy

I want you to know that the Bible says you're in a battle. Now Jesus Himself, the Head of the Church, teaches you how to fight the devil.

God says in the Bible also through Paul that you better know who your enemy is, and you better put on the whole armor of God so that you might be able to stand against the wiles of the devil. (See Ephesians 6:11-18.) You have to stand against the wiles of the devil. Wiles! The devil's wild, crazy as a bat! He's wild.

I've worked in penitentiaries and mental institutions for years. You talk about crazy, I mean the devil is goofy. I've worked in penitentiaries where they gave me a room and the prisoners would just sit around. I'd have a question and answer session for an hour. Most of them don't know why they're in there.

I asked a young man, "How long you in here for?"

"Twenty-five years."

"What did you do?"

"Well, I'm in here for rape."

"Who did you rape?"

"A 70 year old woman."

"How old are you?"

"Twenty-four."

I said, "Now you're a sharp looking young man. You could get most any girl. Why would you rape a 70 year-old woman? Why would you do that?"

"I don't know; something made me do it."

I'd ask another one, "How many years do you have?"

"Fifteen."

"What are you in here for?"

"I'm a bank robber."

"What made you rob the bank? Are you lazy? Don't you want to work?"

"I just got hung up with the wrong crowd I guess, and started drinking and something got in me."

It's the same way with all of them; they don't even know why they're in there. They know something did it.

But every time they walk them down those long corridors and open the steel door and push them in their cell and lock it and walk off—some in for 20 years, 10 years, 35 years, 50 years—they stand there and say, "Well this is stupid. Why am I in here? What made me do that? How dumb can you get?"

They don't even know why they're in there. I start telling them that the devil did it and unless I can get that thing out of them and get them filled up with God they'll do the same thing when they get out of there. But 80-85% of them go back in there again.

It's good to minister in penitentiaries. Most of the prisoners are pretty nice fellows; they really are. They just listened to the devil. They had nobody to help them; nobody to warn them about the devil. They don't even know what the devil is. When you start pointing out to them how the devil operates they say, "Yeah, that had to be the devil."

It's good to teach people about Jesus, but you better also teach them about the devil and how to combat him.

The Easy Way to Fight the Devil

I tell you, Jesus has the perfect solution and the perfect way to fight the devil. And He wants to teach you how to do it. It's very simple but you have to do what God says.

Let's look at Matthew chapter 4. You will see from the Bible how Jesus fought the devil. He told me to teach you how He fought the devil and to tell you that you better learn and learn quickly to fight the devil the same way He did. Do you understand what I'm telling you?

Let me say that again so you won't forget it.

Jesus told me to tell you plainly several years ago when He showed me this, that He wanted me to teach you how He fought the devil. And He told me to tell you to learn quickly how to fight the devil the same way He did.

The Lord Jesus Christ is an example for us. We're supposed to fight the devil the same way that Jesus fought the devil. Now this is the easy way to fight the devil. There's nothing that the devil can do with the Word of God, nothing.

All through the New Testament Jesus offers you things and tells you about all the benefits you can have, but you can't have them unless you believe the Word and claim the benefits, chapter and verse.

When you claim something, remind God of the chapter and verse that you're standing on and claiming in Jesus' name. Remind God. Quote the Bible to God. God likes for you to quote the Bible to Him. God likes for you to go to Him and say, "God, I come in Jesus' name. The Bible says chapter so and so, verse so and so that this is mine." Start quoting what it says, claim it in Jesus' name, thank God for it, and walk off like you got it. Boy, I tell you God loves that kind of praying. Why? Because He knows you've been reading the Bible and you haven't just dreamed up a bunch of things in your mind.

The Battle Begins

God left the Bible on the earth to get your thinking straightened out. And I'm going to teach you the fourth chapter of the book of Matthew to get your thinking straightened out on how to fight the devil. If you can't follow the example of the Lord Jesus Christ you might as well hang it up, go home and get under the house. You'll never be in victory anyway.

Now the battle always starts after the Spirit of the Lord comes upon you. That's when the battle starts. That's the way the devil operates.

A lot of times, a young man that doesn't know anything about God will go out with three or four young boys on a Saturday night and try to pick up girls if they don't have a date. They'll try to pick up girls. That's just the way young men are. And a lot of times it's hard to pick up girls. When they get saved and baptized in the Holy Ghost and start working for God, then girls try to pick them up all the time. Isn't that wild? A young man doesn't know God and he goes out on a Saturday night and tries to pick up a girl and some Saturday nights he can't even pick one up. He gets saved and baptized with the Holy Ghost and there will be six girls trying to pick him up. The devil's nuts man, I'm telling you.

After the Spirit of the Lord comes into you, then the battle begins. That's the reason it's very important to you to know the Word of God. Learn to do things like Jesus did them.

"Then was Jesus led up of the Spirit (this was after
John baptized Him) **into the wilderness to be tempted of
the devil. And when he had fasted forty days and forty
nights, he was afterward an hungred. And when the
tempter came to him** (that means the devil), **he said** (the
devil did), **If."** About 2/3 of his conversation with you will
be IF so and so, IF so and so. Now notice what the jerk
says right here. **"If thou be the Son of God** (If thou be the
Son of God. He knew that Jesus was the Son of God; he
was in heaven with Him), **command that these stones be
made bread."**

Why?

Well Jesus had been fasting forty days and forty nights.

"But he (Jesus) answered and said, IT IS WRITTEN."

Say that out loud, IT IS WRITTEN. Say that again,
IT IS WRITTEN.

Now that's your answer for the rest of your life.

Do you understand that?

That's your answer for the rest of your life. In the
Bible is where all of your answers are. Whatever is written
in there, that's what you've got.

Now you might say, "Well it's in the Bible but I don't
have it." You haven't claimed it then. You have to learn
how to apply the Word of God. The Word of God doesn't
work for you unless you apply it.

Let me break it right down for you so I can teach it to
you. When's the last time you read the Bible to the devil?
Every Christian should read the Bible to the devil. If you'll

read the Bible to the devil he will never be able to steal the patience of God away from you. And for you to possess patience is so important in your life. I don't mean have it every once in a while, I mean to POSSESS patience.

The devil will bombard your mind and give you all kinds of excuses why you're not going to receive something from God. But if you'll just stand steadfast with patience and say, "Well it is written devil, that it's mine. The Bible says I have it"; that will get rid of temptations in your mind quicker than anything else. Just say it boldly: "The Bible says I have it."

He Won't Quit the First Time

Now he won't quit the first time. The Lord told me to tell you and to show you in the Bible that he won't quit the first time.

Suppose you go to a service and walk up to the front and say, "Lay your hands on me Brother, I want to be healed." Someone lays his hands on you and maybe the power of God comes on you so strong that you fall flat on the floor and the healing power of God just surges through you. If you think you're going to get away with that with the devil, I've got news for you. I guarantee you the next day or in just two or three days the devil will come to you and tell you, you didn't get healed. And he'll try to make symptoms show up again. When the symptoms come on you again, that's when he tells you, "You didn't get it. You are not healed. You did not get it. You did not get it."

Now that's when you need to rise up, right then, and say, "The Bible says I did. It is written in the Bible that I did."

And if he keeps on bugging you, just turn the Bible to Mark 16 and read it to him. Say, "Devil, Jesus said right here to lay hands on the sick and they shall recover. I walked up there by faith, and I got that Brother to lay his hands on me. He laid his hands on me so therefore, I got it. It's mine. It is written in the Bible that it's mine. I've already got it."

Why?

Because that Scripture was fulfilled. It is written that you have it. It is written. It says to lay hands on the sick and they shall recover. The moment that he laid his hands on you, I don't care how you felt, you were healed. That split second when he laid his hands on you, you were healed.

Why?

Because it is written; that's the way it is.

Let's read on in verse 4: **"But he (Jesus) answered and said, It is written, Man shall not live by bread alone, but by every word that proceedeth out of the mouth of God."**

See, He said by every word, every word, EVERY word that proceedeth out of the mouth of God. That's the reason you need the whole Bible. You need to study the Bible and find out what it says.

He'll Be Back

Don't think the devil is just going to walk off and leave you alone and never come back and tempt you again, because I've got news for you: he'll be back.

Now the fifth verse: **"Then the devil taketh him up into the holy city, and setteth him on a pinnacle of the temple, And saith unto him. . . ."** This is what the Lord told me to point out to you, look what the devil says: "IF THOU BE THE SON OF GOD." See, he said the same dumb thing, IF.

Now notice the devil mocking Jesus here: **"If thou be the Son of God, cast thyself down: for it is written, He shall give his angels charge concerning thee: and in their hands they shall bear thee up, lest at any time thou dash thy foot against a stone."** Yeah, the devil said, it is written.

Now this is the second time the Lord told me to tell you that you must obey the Bible and do what He did. Don't let your mind wander away from God's Word and come at it a different way. Jesus told me to point out to you what He did and teach YOU to do what He did.

In the seventh verse, **"Jesus said unto him** (the devil), **IT IS WRITTEN."**

Say that out loud, IT IS WRITTEN. Say it again, IT IS WRITTEN. Now remember as long as you live that that is what you always say to the devil. It is written, devil. It is written, devil. Get your Bible and read the Bible to the devil. When you open up your Bible say, "Devil, I do have it because it is written and I'm going to read it to you right now." And then read it to him.

The Word Works

I ministered to a lady in San Antonio, Texas several years ago. She came forward one morning in a service. She had a great responsibility in a big corporation. She had a lot of people working for her. She said the pressure on her was so great that she could hardly stand it.

I ministered to her what it was and God really moved on her and set her mind free. Her mind was so clear and she was weeping and crying and rejoicing in the Lord.

She came up later and said, "Brother Norvel, I've been a Christian for years but the pressure on me as far as my job is concerned is so heavy I can't hold onto this feeling. If I could just stay like I am right now! When I go back into my office and that pressure comes back on me, my mind gets so messed up and confused."

I said, "Do you know what that is?"

She said, "What?"

"It's the devil," I said. "The devil comes to confuse your mind. Now I'm going to tell you what to do. I want you to read the Bible to the devil. You have received the joy of the Lord according to Mark 11:24. We have prayed and you have received. Jesus said whatever you believed for when you prayed, believe that you received it and you shall get it. You will get it. All right, you believed and now you've got it and you know you've got it. Don't you let the devil rob you of the joy. Now, I want you to take your Bible to work with you tomorrow and lay it on your desk. When the devil comes to you, tomorrow or the next day or whenever he shows up, Jesus says he always comes (Mark 4:15), take your Bible; open it up and read it to the devil. Tell him that you HAVE RECEIVED, not GOING TO. YOU HAVE RECEIVED. Just sit there at your desk and say, 'I've got the joy of the Lord. I have received the joy of the Lord in my mind and in my spirit. I possess joy. I won't accept confusion. No pressure can put confusion on me. My mind belongs to God in Jesus' name. You'll not rob me devil of this joy.' And start reading the Bible to him."

She came back to church a day or two later and jumped up one night and started testifying, rejoicing and shouting. Just shouting right there in the service!

She said, "I never have seen anything like that in my life. You never could have made me believe that something that simple could have worked like that. The devil tried to come back and confuse me and mess me up, just a few hours after I got to work. I did exactly what Brother Norvel told me to do. I took the Bible and laid it on my desk, open. When he came right at my desk, I said, 'No devil, you're not going to rob me of the joy. The pressure is not going to have any effect on me. I've got the joy of the Lord and you're not going to rob me. It is written in the Bible, I have the joy of the Lord.' I read the Bible to him. I said, 'Listen, devil, to what the Bible says.' Then I began to read it to him.

"I'm telling you people, it works. The devil left. I sat there all day with the joy of the Lord in my mind, and my mind clear. All the problems came in on me, all the secretaries, all the work like it always does at one time, just continually, but I just waded right through it calmly. Glory to God! It works! It really works!"

You're not supposed to let the pressures of the world rob you of the joy of the Lord. Listen, the devil wants to do it. He wants to rob you. But you don't have to let him. Tell him like Jesus did the second time, "It is written." Jesus said, **"It is written again, Thou shalt not tempt the Lord thy God"** (verse 7).

You Need the Word

Remember, the devil always comes back; he's not dead. So you need the Word of God and the name of Jesus as long as you live on this earth. Don't think you'll get to be a strong Christian sometime and the devil won't ever tempt you again. Sometimes he will leave you for several weeks, or even for several months. But don't you ever forget, he's going to come again one of these times—maybe through your child, or your business or something else—and try to mess you up.

> Again, the devil taketh him up into an exceeding high mountain, and sheweth him all the kingdoms of the world, and the glory of them; And saith unto him, All these things will I give thee, if thou wilt fall down and worship me.

He offered Jesus the whole world, but he offers you and me a whiskey bottle and X-rated movies—big deal.

94

The devil offered Jesus the whole world. He doesn't offer you and me anything but a bunch of junk.

The tenth verse is the climax of it. Jesus told me to show you and teach you that you've got to get mad at the devil. You've got to get tired and fed up with his temptations, then tell him what to do.

> Then saith Jesus unto him, Get thee hence, Satan: for it is written, Thou shalt worship the Lord thy God, and him only shalt thou serve.

What did He say?

Jesus said to the devil, **"Get thee hence Satan for it is written."** Now remember, every time, you must say, IT IS WRITTEN; IT IS WRITTEN; IT IS WRITTEN. It is written in the Bible that I've got it. It's rightfully mine. It's mine. It is written.

What does that mean?

That means that you fight the devil with the Bible. You use Jesus' name and come against him and use the Bible. Quote the Bible to the devil. Make up your mind. Be determined.

Then What Happens

What happens when you just keep telling the devil in his face, over and over and over and over again, "It is written devil. It is written"?

I'm glad you asked.

The eleventh verse shows you exactly what happens to you, and the Lord told me to tell you it will happen to you exactly the same way it happened to Him IF you'll do the same thing He did.

"Then the devil leaveth him." That moment when the devil leaveth him, glory to God, **"and behold, angels came and ministered unto him."** Angels came and got around Him and began to minister unto Him—angels did. If you'll stand and resist the devil in Jesus' name, tell him what the Bible says, he'll leave you. If you keep on quoting the Bible to him and telling him, "it is written," he'll leave. Then the angels will come and begin to minister to you. I guarantee you, the angels will come and begin to minister to you: Praise God forever!

But you have to stand in the devil's face and learn how to fight him. You have to stand in the devil's face and quote the Bible to him. He'll bombard your mind and dog your tracks as long as you live, if you'll allow him to do it. But you have to stand up steadfast and say, "It is written. The Bible says I have it. The Bible says I have it. The Bible says I have it." If you can get a deaf man to do that his ears will pop open.

But of course I understand the problem is, getting people to do it. It only works for people that do it. The fourth chapter in the book of Matthew doesn't work for people just because they read it. It works for those and only those that do it. The devil only leaves people that stand like Jesus did in the face of the devil and say, "It is written Satan." But you have to SAY that. Don't just think it.

You think, well I'm going to hunt a good spiritual service to go to. Well, that's good, I'm not knocking that. You need to go to good spiritual services. But see, you're only in service a little while on Sunday and Wednesday. What are you going to do on Tuesday afternoon at 2 o'clock? What are you going to do on Friday at 11:30 at night? The devil's not dead on Thursday morning, you know. But you have to understand the Word of God works for you all the time, not just part of the time, all the time. The Bible will stick closer to you than a brother. The Bible works for you all the time, 24 hours a day, every day; but only for those that obey it.

I tell you, God gives you life, but you've got to find it. And you can't find it by just watching Gunsmoke on T.V. You find it by opening up the Bible and studying it. Ask the Holy Ghost to unfold it to you and to show you what you need. He will, because He is the great teacher. Praise God forever! You can have what you believe the Bible for.

When you look the devil in the face and hold the Bible up to him and say, "It is written devil. Devil, it is written. Jesus said I could have the desires of my heart. I am a believer; I'm not a doubter," the devil will leave you in Jesus' name. Then the angels of the Lord will come and minister to you. Glory be to God!

Now, Do the Word

If you'll just be honest now, you might say, "Yes the devil has been trying to mess me up. And I see it; I see it. It is written in the Bible that there is victory for me. It is written in the Bible I don't have to put up with this mountain."

Do you want to get rid of that dumb mountain?

Begin to confess with your mouth: "It is written in the Bible, I have victory. I've got the victory. It is written, I've got the victory. It is written, the victory is mine. The victory is mine."

The victory is yours because you said it in Jesus' name. The Lord Jesus Christ has bought for you and me the abundant life, not a bunch of junk. Jesus didn't pay the price for you and me to live a junky life and to put up with a bunch of junky stuff. That's not the price that Jesus paid. Jesus paid the price so you could have patience, contentment, peace and joy; that you could stand steadfast and not waver.

You have the nature of God in you and it is not His nature to be climbing over mountains all the time and falling into dumb gullies. You have a right to live in peace. You have a right to have the kind of life that Jesus has offered you. You have that right. You inherited it. You are an heir of God, a joint heir with Jesus Christ. Jesus is complete victory. Receive that peace.

Say it gently to the Lord, "It is written, I do have what I desire in Jesus' name. It is written. Thank You for the Bible because the Word is truth. And only the truth will set me free and keep me free in Jesus' name."

Say, "The words from my lips will be from this day forward, 'Satan you thief, IT IS WRITTEN, I am victory in Jesus' name.'"

WHAT TO DO
FOR HEALING

WHAT TO DO FOR HEALING

As I was preparing to minister on God's healing power one time, God gave me three passages of Scripture that show what the people in the Bible did to receive healing from Him. People today should do these same things.

The Lunatic Son

The first example is in Matthew, chapter 17:

When they were come to the multitude, there came to him a certain man, kneeling down to him (v. 14). The man evidently is coming to Jesus for some kind of help. What did he do when he came to Jesus? He knelt down.

The man said, **Lord, have mercy on my son: for he is a lunatic, and sore vexed: for ofttimes he falleth into the fire, and oft into the water. I brought him to thy disciples, and they could not cure him** (w. 15,16).

Jesus said, **O faithless and perverse generation, how long shall I be with you? how long shall I suffer you? Bring him hither to me** *(v. 17).

The first words Jesus spoke when He heard that His disciples had not been able to cure the lunatic were: *O faithless*. Faithless means "no faith."

Jesus was talking about the disciples; but He told the father to bring his son to Him. Why? Because the father expressed his faith when he knelt down before Jesus and said, "Have mercy on my son." The moment he approached Jesus and spoke in faith, Jesus went to work on his behalf.

Jesus rebuked the devil; and he departed out of him: and the child was cured from that very hour (v.18). What did Jesus do? He rebuked the devil.

"Do you mean, Brother Norvel, that people in mental institutions have devils?" That's right. God doesn't make people sick or crazy.

All good things that come to you and your house come down from heaven. (James 1:17.) All bad things that come to the human race are from Satan—the god of darkness, the god of this world—and his workers, the demons. Jesus and His workers, the angels from heaven, are here to bless you and encourage you to believe the Bible.

The Bible says, **The child was cured from that very hour.** Can you imagine all the years of torment that child must have gone through? But he was completely normal in *that very hour*—in sixty minutes or less!

The Devil-Possessed Daughter

The second Scripture God gave me about an incident of healing is Matthew 15:21-28:

Jesus went thence, and departed into the coasts of Tyre and Sidon. And, behold, a woman of Canaan came out of the same coasts, and cried unto him, saying, Have mercy on me, O Lord, thou Son of David; my daughter is grievously vexed with a devil. But he answered her not a word...

Then came she and worshipped him, saying, Lord, help me. But he answered and said, It is not meet to take the children's bread, and to cast it to dogs. And she said, Truth, Lord: yet the dogs eat of the crumbs which fall from their masters' table.

Then Jesus answered and said unto her, O woman, great is thy faith: be it unto thee even as thou wilt. And her daughter was made whole from that very hour.

The disciples tried to send her away, but she worshipped Jesus, telling Him, "You can call me a dog if You want to. I'll even eat the crumbs that fall from Your table because You are my Master, Jesus, and I worship You."

The devil-possessed daughter who needed healing wasn't there in person—she was in another town—but the Spirit of God made her whole again in sixty minutes or less.

I want you to notice something: The healing didn't result until after the woman approached Jesus in reverence and asked Him in faith to help her.

The Leper

The first two Scripture passages God gave me about healing concerned children. This third one from Mark chapter 1, is for the individual:

And there came a leper to him, beseeching him, and kneeling down to him (v. 40). Again, we see that the person who came to Jesus for healing knelt down to Him and worshipped Him.

Today, cancer in certain stages is diagnosed by doctors in this country as incurable. In the days that Jesus walked the earth, leprosy was incurable.

This leper said to Jesus, **If thou wilt, thou canst make me clean** (v. 40). Some people think this statement expresses doubt. At the beginning, it sounds as though it does; but the last part is saying, "You *can* heal me, Jesus." This leper is expressing faith with his mouth.

And Jesus, moved with compassion, put forth his hand, and touched him, and saith unto him, I will; be thou clean. And as soon as he had spoken, immediately the leprosy departed from him, and he was cleansed (vv. 41,42).

They Worshipped and Received

In Matthew 17, the man knelt down before Jesus and said, "Jesus, have mercy on my son. He is a lunatic and is possessed with devils." When they brought the boy to Jesus, he was healed *from that very hour.*

In Matthew 15, the woman knelt down before Jesus and said, "You're my Master, Jesus. I worship You, Lord." Even though her devil-possessed daughter was in another town, she was made whole *from that very hour*.

In Mark 1, the leper knelt down to Jesus and said, *Thou canst make me clean*. When Jesus touched him, he was healed immediately.

In the first two instances, the parents wanted healing and deliverance for their children. In the third, a man wanted healing for himself.

In all three examples, the people sought God in the same way: They approached Jesus through worship by kneeling down before Him; and they expressed faith to Him through their words.

God responded in each case by healing them immediately.

Know That Jesus Heals

To receive healing, you must know, once and for all, that Jesus heals people today.

I'm not saying the devil won't attack you. He will. He will tell you: "You have been a Christian for so long. You know how much the Lord loves you. If He wanted to heal you, He would." That's not in the Scriptures. The Bible says God wants to heal everybody.

You also have to get it settled from the Bible that healing is for you . Jesus is no respecter of persons. (Acts 10:34.) He didn't love the people in the Bible more than

He loves you. He isn't like other human beings who love some people, but don't love others.

Jesus doesn't want a member of your family to be sick the rest of his life. He wants to heal *you* and He wants to heal your family.

You must also get your belief settled that the price for your healing has already been paid. You don't have to wait for an evangelist to come to town to pray for you. You can have your healing now.

How To Approach God For Healing

Two things play an important role in how God manifests Himself and the amount of power He imparts to you to give you what you have asked for:

1. How you approach God.
2. What you say with your mouth.

Ask in Faith

The Holy Spirit will begin to move upon you when He finds favor in what you are doing. If you do exactly what the Bible says to do, then the Holy Spirit will encourage you because you are basing your actions on Scripture.

The way to get Jesus to manifest Himself is to ask for what you want in faith.

All through the New Testament, people boldly walked up to Jesus and said, "I want to be healed." There is no Scripture, from Matthew to Revelation, that says

Jesus ever turned anyone away. He never said, "No. I'm not going to heal you." He touched anyone who asked Him for help and said, "Your faith has healed you." The deaf heard; the blind saw; the lame walked.

You have to show Jesus your faith; then He will heal you.

Know How To Receive His Healing Power

The same healing power that flowed through Jesus to open blind eyes and deaf ears is available for you today.

God's divine healing power is a substance exactly like His saving power. It flows automatically like a river, all through the air and everywhere in heaven. It is so strong that it can keep everything well.

After your spirit has been reborn by the Spirit of God, it is no longer a natural spirit. The Holy Ghost, who does all the work on the earth today, lives inside you. Whenever you believe the Bible, you enable God through the Holy Ghost to release His divine healing power (or whatever is needed) from heaven to your spirit here on earth. That healing power then flows from your spirit into your body and brings the healing or the miracle you need.

Several years ago, God put His healing power in my hands, and it has been there ever since. When it happened, I was speaking in Pennsylvania at a banquet in a Holiday Inn ballroom. The room was so full that people were standing around the walls .

A nice-looking fellow walked up to the front and said, "I'm a Full Gospel businessman here in town. I didn't know what was wrong with me until I heard you talk tonight. My ears have been stopped up for years and there is a knot in my belly about half as big as a football. I know now that there is a connection between the knot and my ears."

The Lord said to me, "Cast that deaf spirit out of him."

When an evil spirit has hold of a person, it won't let go very easily unless you command it to go with authority in Jesus' name. Then it has to go! It would inhabit a person for forty years if somebody didn't command it to leave.

I walked over to the man and said, "You foul deaf spirit, in Jesus' name, I command you to come out of him!"

The moment the Lord told me to cast out that deaf spirit, He put a great measure of His healing power in my hands. The man fell straight forward, face down on the floor. You would have thought all his teeth would have been knocked out, but they weren't.

Then he bounced and fell back down again. That impact could have broken his nose, but it didn't.

Again, he bounced up off the floor and fell back. This time he laid there real quiet for about sixty seconds. Then his mouth opened and a little squeaky sound like a mouse began to come out. It got louder, sounding like a big rat, and finally sounded like a screaming hyena.

In a little while the man shook his head and pushed himself up off the floor. He acted as if he had been hit in the head with a stick, but both ears had popped open and the knot in his stomach was gone!

The man had stepped up while I was still speaking. I hadn't given the invitation yet. Almost everybody at the banquet was from that town and they knew him. When the people—about 150 of them—saw that his ears had popped open and that the knot had disappeared, they jumped out of their seats and started running toward me, saying, "Pray for me!"

As I reached out and began to pray, it was as though the wind of God had come into my hands! People were lying all around on the floor, including denominational pastors. God baptized them in the Holy Ghost; and the moment they hit the floor, they started talking in tongues!

About five minutes later an old man walked up to me, stepping around the people who were lying crosswise and on top of each other on the floor. He told me what a blessing I was to him and said, "This is the first time in many years that I've seen this old-time power from heaven."

Do you know where you get that kind of power? From the Word of God.

Even though God may channel a great degree of healing power through you, you may not always feel it. Don't base whether or not you've been healed on your feelings.

Fred Price, pastor of Crenshaw Christian Center in Los Angeles, has a healing ministry in which about 98 percent of the people get healed. Why? Because he doesn't allow his congregation to operate according to their feelings.

After fifteen years in the ministry, Fred had about 350 people in his church. When he began to teach healing and faith from the Bible, his congregation grew in four years to 2200!

I have seen Fred pray for 100 people without anybody feeling anything. When he asks those who got healed to raise their hands, everybody except maybe one person holds up his hand. He then spends about ten minutes showing them from the Bible why they are already healed. His church draws people because everybody gets healed.

Fred teaches those 2200 people to believe God for everything. They open their Bibles and they tell the devil, and anybody else who asks, that they have what they are believing for—no matter how they feel or what they see.

Believe God's Word

Jesus said, **All things are possible to him that believeth** (Mark 9:23). God requires every person to believe the Bible and obey the Scriptures as they are written.

When God called me years ago, He said, "I want you to teach the Bible to the Church. I want you to teach them some things I've taught you. Everything I teach you, I'll give you a Scripture for."

Remember this: I don't have a "Norvel Hayes Gospel." You may think speaking in tongues and healing are strange because you have never been taught about them, but they are still in the Bible.

Maybe you've tried to make yourself believe in healing, but you can't. Maybe you've been taught another way for so long that it doesn't make any difference to you what the Bible says. But it does make a difference! **Faith cometh by hearing, and hearing by the word of God** (Rom. 10:17).

God doesn't go by what you have been taught. He goes according to what He has given you in the Bible. Read the Bible for yourself. Believe it on your own. God will bless you.

Believe and Confess

Hebrews 11:1 says, **Faith is the substance of things hoped for, the evidence of things not seen**. Regardless of how you feel, when you believe God, you have the substance: your faith, your believing.

Boldly confess what you are believing for, and God will work strongly for you. (2 Chron. 6:9.) He will give you everything you ask Him for. (John 15:7.)

Talk as though you've got it, and it will come. If you have to stop and think how to say it, then you don't really believe you've got it.

Nearly all Full Gospel Christians will say, "I believe that Jesus is going to heal me someday." But He is not obligated to do it as long as you talk like that. You are talking words of doubt.

With God "someday" never comes. Faith is right now. Stick your teeth into what you are believing for just like a tiger would stick his teeth into a piece of meat. Say boldly: "I've got it because God's Word says I have. It's mine now. I see it. I'm not *going* to get it; *I've got it right now!*"

James 1:6,7 says no one should think that he will receive anything from God if he wavers. To receive healing, you must have the "Abraham kind" of faith: be patient without doubting.

There was a time when my daughter had backslidden from God and was involved in dope and drugs. During the two years I prayed for her, she got even worse. After a healing service I had conducted in San Antonio, Texas, God told me my faith was wrong where my daughter was concerned. He said I was doubting.

In the meeting that night, people were healed all over the auditorium; but God said I had been doubting Him. How could that be? I found out that your faith can be strong in one area and weak in another.

God told me that the darkness over my daughter was too strong for her to come back to Him through her own faith; but He said that my faith could enable Him to visit her.

Attend a Church That Believes in Healing

If you want to be healed, you have to go to a church where the people believe in divine healing power. Your friends may be precious Christian people; but if their knowledge of God's healing power isn't strong, you'd better not follow their advice about healing.

Southern Baptists have strong faith in salvation. If they ever memorize all the healing verses in the Bible and turn their faith loose on the sick people in town, everybody they pray for would probably get healed. But they don't have any faith in healing.

My family was Southern Baptist, and my mother loved Jesus. The Spirit of God would come on her with a glow of power that made her look like an angel. When that happened, she would shout without shame wherever she was—in a church or in a field.

Mother believed in God, but she didn't believe in divine healing. She died of cancer at 37. My brother, who was a football player in high school, died at 19 of Bright's disease, a disease of the kidneys.

There was no reason for them to die. Cancer is a lie, and God can give you new kidneys; but if you don't know that, you will suffer with your old infected kidneys (or whatever problem the devil puts on you).

If somebody had given my sweet Southern Baptist mother some of these healing verses, she would have believed them because she was open to God.

What to Do for the Healing of Others

Be willing to do anything the Holy Spirit tells you to do. He may lead you into an unusual ministry that will get people saved and healed—people who otherwise would be lost and sick.

God will do anything with people who have His joy and power in them.

I heard a man and wife testify at a convention about an unusual ministry God had given them: cleaning filthy houses.

These are respectable, nice-looking people who live in a fine home; but every morning they go to skid row. The

Lord shows them a filthy house that He wants them to clean. They go to the door and ask if they can scrub and clean at no charge—just to show their love. The people usually let them come in.

They never try to shove Jesus down the people's throats. While they take their time scrubbing and cleaning, they show their love and happily sing to the Lord.

Usually by noon the people are feeling convicted for the sins they have committed and begin to ask questions: "What are you people made out of? Why are you doing this? Because you love us? You don't even know us. How can you love us?

They answer, "Jesus loves you, and because Jesus is in us, He has given us His love for you." They win hundreds of souls to God through their cleaning ministry.

How To Pray For Healing

When you pray for healing, kneel down before Jesus and show God your faith. If you need a miracle in your life or healing for any kind of affliction in your body, kneel before Jesus and say, "Jesus, You are my healer."

Stick to the Scriptures when you pray. Don't try to dream up something new.

No matter what condition you may be in, God loves you just as much as He loved the people in the Bible. When you pay the same price as those people did, you will get the same results.

Kneel down before God. Cry out for Him to have mercy on you, and God Almighty will heal you. Why? Because the Bible says He will.

I Pray This for You…

In the name of the Lord Jesus Christ, I pray for you now.

I rise up against the devil and his power over you. In Jesus' name, I command Satan to let you go free! I command the foul devils that have wrecked your life and bound you up with sickness and disease to let you go free!

Jesus said you can't come to Him unless the Spirit draws you, so I pray now that the Holy Spirit will melt your heart and make you sensitive to God.

I command all darkness to flee from you. I pray that the light of God will shine on you and the Spirit of the Living God will wash you white as snow. I accept it in faith as done now, in Jesus' name.

Thank You, Jesus, that You hear my prayer.

Know That He Hears Your Prayers

The Spirit of God once showed me how you can know when your prayer has been answered. After you have prayed long enough, the Holy Ghost will begin to laugh inside you. Joy will start bubbling up supernaturally.

God loves you and He wants you to know it! Approach Him in reverence and faith, and He will lead you!

Healing Scriptures

My son, attend to my words; incline thine ear unto my sayings. Let them not depart from thine eyes; keep them in the midst of thine heart. For they are life unto those that find them, and health to all their flesh.

Proverbs 4:20–22

Behold, I will bring health and cure, and I will heal them, and will reveal unto them the abundance of peace and truth.

Jeremiah 33:6

…Thus saith the Lord, the God of David thy father, I have heard thy prayer, I have seen thy tears: behold, I will heal thee.

2 Kings 20:5

Be not wise in thine own eyes: fear the Lord, and depart from evil. It will be health (medicine) *to thy navel, and marrow* (refreshment) *to thy bones.*

Proverbs 3:7,8

And ye shall serve the Lord your god, and he shall bless thy bread, and thy water; and I will take sickness from the midst of thee.

Exodus 23:25

Now when the sun was setting, all they that had any sick with divers diseases brought them unto him; and he laid hands on every one of them, and healed them.

Luke 4:40

And Jesus went forth, and saw a great multitude, and was moved with compassion toward them, and he healed their sick.

Matthew 14:14

...they brought unto him many that were possessed with devils: and he cast out the spirits with his word, and healed all that were sick.

Matthew 8:16

...they brought unto him all sick people that were taken with divers diseases and torments...and he healed them.

Matthew 4:24

And the prayer of faith shall save the sick, and the Lord shall raise him up.

James 5:15

Who his own self bare our sins in his own body on the tree, that we, being dead to sins, should live unto righteousness: by whose stripes ye were healed.

1 Peter 2:24

He was wounded for our transgressions, he was bruised for our iniquities: the chastisement of our peace was upon him; and with his stripes we are healed.

Isaiah 53:5

And when I passed by thee, and saw thee polluted in thine own blood, I said unto thee when thou wast in thy blood, Live: yea, I said unto thee when thou wast in thy blood, Live.

Ezekiel 16:6

...I will put none of these diseases upon thee...for I am the Lord that healeth thee.

Exodus 15:26

Bless the Lord, O my soul, and forget not all his benefits: Who forgiveth all thine iniquities; who healeth all thy diseases.

Psalm 103:2,3

For I will restore health unto thee, and I will heal thee of thy wounds, saith the Lord.

Jeremiah 30:17

WHY YOU SHOULD SPEAK IN TONGUES

WHY YOU SHOULD
SPEAK IN TONGUES

According to the New Testament, Jesus wants to baptize everybody on earth with the Holy Ghost. He wants everybody on earth to speak in other tongues. That's what the New Testament says, not just in one place, but in several places. In 1 Corinthians 14 the Apostle Paul said, **…forbid not to speak with tongues** (v. 39).

Unless you allow Jesus to baptize you in the Holy Ghost, you won't ever receive power from on High to do the works of God.

Paul said you pray in tongues to edify yourself. **He that speaketh in an unknown tongue edifieth himself** (1 Cor. 14:4). To edify means build yourself up. Speaking in tongues builds you to the point that you can believe God instead of circumstances.

Circumstances don't have anything to do with God. He will remove circumstances if you'll just believe Him.

The way you believe is the way you talk. What you're believing comes out of your innermost being. The words you speak come from your heart, your inner man. The words you speak show exactly the shape that your inner man is in.

You are what you say, and you will never be anything else. The condition of your own personal life today is the result of what you said yesterday. By "yesterday" I mean your past life, your past meditation, your past attitude toward God and the Bible.

There is complete victory for you if you will read the Bible and believe it—believe those words came out of the mouth of God for you! If you fight and wrestle with what God says, you will miss out on what He wants for your life.

If you never speak in tongues, Jesus will still love you. You can go to heaven and never speak in tongues. To go to heaven, all you have to do is be born again by the Spirit of God. If you have received Jesus Christ as the Lord of your life, when you die, the angels will be waiting to receive your spirit and take you to heaven.

You may be saying, "But what good is speaking in tongues? They don't teach that in my church. Why should I want to speak in some language I don't understand?"

Let me ask you a question: "When you pray, do you pray to yourself?" No. You pray to God.

The Bible says, **For he that speaketh in an unknown tongue speaketh not unto men, but unto God** (1 Cor. 14:2). By speaking in tongues, you speak directly to God, bypassing all human reasonings.

Speaking in tongues gives you power to believe the Bible. Unless you have faith, you can't believe what the Bible says and you won't do what it says.

The last command Jesus gave to the Church was for her to believe the Gospel. We are to stand before the world and boldly say, "I'm a believer of the Lord Jesus Christ."

God let me know one time that some people don't get their prayers answered because they don't bow down before Him and worship Him as God. They jump over the first commandment that God gave to Moses on Mount Sinai for the human race to live by. They jump over that commandment and get hung up in religion. They get busy in church, doing this and that, but they don't take the time to bow down before God and spend time alone, worshipping Him.

God wants to be your God and He wants you to be His child. He wants you to love Him like a Father. He wants to love you through the pages of His Word, the Bible. He won't love you through your head.

Oh, how beautiful it is when you say, "God, I'm just going to read the New Testament and believe what You have told me in it. Whatever You have said, that's exactly what I'm going to believe. I'm going to act like it's true, regardless of how I feel."

When I reached that point and made that decision, my whole life changed. God changed me into a new man.

Bearing Fruit

God wants you to know who you are in Him. He wants you to know you have inherited everything in the New Testament. All of it is for you! When you stop listening to humans and start standing on the Word just because God said it, you will become a tree that will bear fruit.

There are lots of Christians who have never won a soul to Jesus. They could win souls every week if they would just do it. It's so easy.

Do *you* want to win souls for Jesus? To do it, you need to receive power from on High.

Soulwinning won't seem easy when you first start because you haven't been used to it. You need to pray in the Spirit and get yourself built up; then doing the things of God will be normal to you.

If someone comes to you in bad shape, all messed up, the first thing you have to do is take authority over the darkness that's trying to wreck his life. You have to take authority over the devil. With the Spirit of God in you, you have the power of God to do it.

God's Word is so powerful. It's sharper than a two-edged sword. (Heb. 4:12.) With the baptism of the Holy Spirit, you have God's power and God's Word working in you.

You have to stand on God's Word for that person's salvation and break the power of the devil in Jesus' name. Bind the power of darkness. Tell the devil, "No, you're not taking this person to hell. I'm not going to let you! I break your power in Jesus' name."

As you stand steadfast in faith, you'll see God's power deal with that person.

If you want to bear fruit in this life, receive the baptism of the Holy Ghost. Learn how to pray in the Spirit (in other tongues). Paul said, **I thank my God, I speak with tongues more than ye all** (1 Cor. 14:18).

You might say, "But Paul also said it's better to speak five words in your own language than ten thousand words in an unknown tongue." That's true, but you have to read that verse in its setting.

> I thank my God, I speak with tongues more than ye all:
>
> Yet in the church I had rather speak five words with my understanding, that by my voice I might teach others also, than ten thousand words in an unknown tongue.
>
> 1 Corinthians 14:18,19

Here Paul was talking about teaching people in the Church. You will learn much more if I say, "Jesus loves you," than if I get behind the pulpit and speak twenty thousand words in an unknown tongue. I can't teach you anything by speaking in tongues. You have to understand what I'm saying if you're going to learn anything.

One reason Jesus wants to baptize you with the Holy Ghost and have you speak in other tongues in your

125

personal life is so that you'll be able to bear fruit. With the Holy Ghost, you'll have the power to go out and tell people that Jesus loves them.

What happens to a person if he doesn't bear fruit?

You may think that as long as you're living a half-way decent life, you will get by. But you won't get by—not with God. You will have to answer to Him for everything.

God wants to mold you into what He wants you to be. He wants to use your mouth, your lips, your personality.

One Sunday morning I was to teach an adult class. God woke me up at six o'clock and said:

"You tell them I made Moses exactly like I wanted him and I did through him exactly what I wanted to do. Tell them I made Samson exactly like I wanted him. I put strength and power in him because I wanted to. Tell them I made Billy Graham just like I wanted him.

"I've never made two personalities alike. I've got a job for each person to do. If he doesn't do that job, it will never get done because nobody else is like him."

It's up to you as an individual to find out what God wants you to do. Do what you can for the Kingdom of God. Nobody else is going to do it like you can. They will do what God wants them to do, but they don't have your face, your personality. They don't have it, and they never will have it.

God made you like He wants you. There are certain people in the world that only you can win. Maybe a person you can't win, I can. Maybe a person I can't win, you can.

Let God mold you. Be a tree that will bear good fruit.

The Comforter

Jesus lived His life on earth and went into His ministry under the power that God gave Him. He died on the cross and rose again just like God intended for Him to.

Before He went to the cross, Jesus told His disciples, **I will pray the Father, and he shall give you another Comforter, that he may abide with you for ever** (John 14:16).

God sent the Holy Ghost—the third party from the throne of God. The Holy Ghost thinks just like God thinks. He is a divine personality sent from the throne of God to live in you.

In His first appearance for the human race, the Holy Ghost came to only the 120 people in the Upper Room.

> And when the day of Pentecost was fully come, they were all with one accord in one place. And suddenly there came a sound from heaven as of a rushing mighty wind, and it filled all the house where they were sitting.
>
> And there appeared unto them cloven tongues like as of fire, and it sat upon each of them. And they were all filled with the Holy Ghost, and began to speak with other tongues, as the Spirit gave them utterance.
>
> Acts 2:1-4

What God did for those 120 people, He will do for anybody. It doesn't make any difference what color they are, what size they are, where they come from, or how much money they have. God doesn't care. If the thousands of people outside the Upper Room in Jerusalem had been praying like those 120, the Holy Ghost would have come on all of them!

Receive By Faith

You can receive the baptism of the Holy Ghost without an immediate supernatural manifestation.

When I tried to receive the baptism of the Holy Ghost, I had made up my mind that I wouldn't say anything until some supernatural power came on me and made me talk in tongues. For over a year, nothing happened.

Then I began to think something was wrong with me. Everybody else was receiving. I said, "Lord, I know the Holy Spirit is in me. I know I've been born again. If I died today, I know I would go to heaven. But, Lord, I want to receive the power of the Holy Ghost. Then I won't be ashamed to cast out devils, pray for the sick, pass out tracts, and pray for my friends and neighbors. I can tell them the truth in love and in power, then watch You perform Your Word. Lord, I need more power."

I couldn't receive the baptism of the Holy Ghost because I was waiting for some supernatural power to take over my tongue and make me talk. It never did.

Then I began to study the Bible on the subject of faith. In Hebrews 11:1 I found God's definition of faith: **Now faith is the substance of things hoped for, the evidence of things not seen.**

If I expected to get the substance, I had to believe that I had already received because now *faith is*. In this case, the substance was the baptism of the Holy Spirit and speaking with other tongues. I had to believe that I had it, even though I couldn't see it or feel it. Faith is the answer we see when we pray.

According to Acts 2:4, *they* began to speak as the Spirit gave them utterance. My part was to speak. The Holy Spirit's part was to give me the utterance. My part was to speak and, according to Hebrews' definition of faith, I had to believe I had it *before* I got it.

Then I read Mark 11:23,24—my foundation Scripture for believing. Jesus said:

> For verily I say unto you, That whosoever shall say unto this mountain, Be thou removed, and be thou cast into the sea; and shall not doubt in his heart, but shall believe that those things which he saith shall come to pass; he shall have whatsoever he saith.
>
> Therefore I say unto you, What things soever ye desire, when ye pray, believe that ye receive them, and ye shall have them.

Does this mean that if I say I believe I receive the baptism in the Holy Ghost, that's what I'll get?

Jesus said, *what things soever ye desire....* I desired to have the baptism of the Holy Ghost so I could receive more power. I had sense enough to know that Jesus doesn't tell lies. He said I was to believe I received when I prayed. I had to cooperate with the Scriptures and do my part.

Acts 2:4 says the people in the Upper Room *began to speak with other tongues* as the Spirit gave them utterance. My part was to begin to speak.

I had studied the Bible and saw that it was true, so one night I just bowed down before the Lord and prayed, "Lord, Your Word says in James 4:2 that we have not because we ask not. I'm asking You tonight, Jesus, to baptize me in the Holy Ghost."

Then I had to put some action to my faith. The book of Acts says it's my responsibility to do the speaking, so I tried to speak. I spoke out some little sounds, not words, and I never did feel anything. But that was enough for me.

On the basis of the Scriptures, I received it by faith. I got up and said, "Thank You, Jesus, for baptizing me in the Holy Ghost."

I didn't feel anything, but I didn't base it on feelings. I based it on the Word of God. If I had based it on feelings, I would still be waiting for that supernatural language to come unto me.

I also followed the instructions Jesus gave in Mark 11:23 by *confessing with my mouth that I had received.* I said, "Thank You, Jesus, for baptizing me in the Holy Ghost."

Before I could even get to my car that night, the devil was saying to me, "Come on now, you didn't get baptized in the Holy Ghost. That wasn't a supernatural language you spoke. You were just mumbling. Stop saying that!"

But I just said, "Thank You, Jesus, for baptizing me in the Holy Ghost."

The devil said, "You didn't receive anything. You're lying, and as a Christian you aren't supposed to lie. Stop saying that!"

I just turned a deaf ear to him and said, "According to Mark 11:23 I can have whatever I say. According to Mark 11:24 if I believe I have it when I pray, I will get it. I have it now, Satan, because I believed I received when I prayed!"

For a month I kept saying over and over again, "Thank You, Jesus, for baptizing me in the Holy Ghost. It was so terrible for that year when I was seeking the Holy Ghost and never could receive. But now I have received the baptism in the Holy Ghost, and it feels so good! I don't base my believing on feelings. My believing is based on Your Word!"

Wherever I was—in my office, my house, my car—I kept saying it, still without any supernatural language coming to me. I hadn't felt a thing. But I was walking by faith, not by feelings.

There is only one way that the things of God will be manifested for you and your family: by faith, by your confession of the Scriptures. Are you willing to make God's Word the foundation of your believing? If you do, God won't fail you.

How I Received

One night God told me to go to a meeting in Chattanooga. When the preacher finished his sermon, he gave the invitation.

131

As I was sitting there, my body suddenly began to get warm. Every part of my body—arms, legs, back, chest, fingers, ears—began to tingle. I felt like there were thousands of little men tickling me inside with soft brushes.

The devil said, "You're having a heart attack!"

I had never felt anything like that before. (I had been blessed—something supernatural.) My body began to turn from hot to warm to hot again, and the tingling sensation got stronger and stronger.

I thought, *Devil, this can't be a heart attack. It feels too good!*

I really didn't know what was happening. I felt like it was God, but I didn't know for sure. Then I thought, *I'll walk out to my car. When I get outside on the sidewalk, this will leave me.*

I walked to my car, but the feeling didn't leave me. I got in my car and started driving through Chattanooga. Then I drove onto the bypass going toward Atlanta and Knoxville. As I was driving, I just praised the Lord. The tingling sensation kept on.

Oh, God, what is this? What's happening to me, Lord?

Then as I drove along, I began to feel real hot deep down in my belly. Slowly, it began to move forward and upward, flowing throughout the rest of my body. Finally, my whole body was hot. I thought my toes were going to jump off my feet!

Then it came up into my throat. It felt so good. I opened my mouth, let the sound come through my voice box, and turned my tongue loose. I thought, *Glory to God forevermore! Here it comes!*

The supernatural language began to come out of my innermost being. I began speaking in tongues! It was a beautiful experience! So beautiful! I had never known such a manifestation from God in all my life. It was wonderful to get saved, but this....

Are You Ready?

Can I ask you boldly without offending you, "Are you ready to speak in tongues?"

The only responsibility of the Holy Spirit to you or anyone else is to give you the utterance like He did on the day of Pentecost. He came to give the utterance, but you do the speaking.

I want you to base your believing on the Scriptures I have given you, and receive by faith as I lead you in this prayer. By faith just speak out any sounds or syllables that rise up within you. Are you ready now?

Dear heavenly Father,

I come before You now with an open heart to receive all You have for me. I have already accepted the Lord Jesus as the Lord and Savior of my life, so now I open myself to receive the power of Your Holy Spirit.

You said in Your Word that if I asked, I would receive, so I ask You now to fill me to overflowing with Your precious Holy Spirit.

I receive Him now by faith and expect to speak with other tongues as He gives me the utterance...

In Jesus' name, Amen.

Scriptures

And I will pray the Father, and he shall give you another Comforter, that he may abide with you for ever; Even the Spirit of truth; whom the world cannot receive, because it seeth him not, neither knoweth him: but ye know him; for he dwelleth with you, and shall be in you.

John 14:16,17

And when the day of Pentecost was fully come, they were all with one accord in one place. And suddenly there came a sound from heaven as of a rushing mighty wind, and it filled all the house where they were sitting. And there appeared unto them cloven tongues like as of fire, and it sat upon each of them. And they were all filled with the Holy Ghost, and began to speak with other tongues, as the Spirit gave them utterance.

Acts 2:1-4

But this is that which was spoken by the prophet Joel; And it shall come to pass in the last days, saith God, I will pour out of my Spirit upon all flesh: and your sons and your daughters shall prophesy, and your young men shall see visions, and your old men shall dream dreams: And on my servants and on my handmaidens I will pour out in those days of my Spirit; and they shall prophesy. (See Joel 2:28.)

Acts 2:16-18

*This Jesus hath God raised up, whereof we all are wit-
nesses. Therefore being by the right hand of God exalted,
and having received of the Father the promise of the
Holy Ghost, he hath shed forth this, which ye now see
and hear.*

Acts 2:32,33

*Then Peter said unto them, Repent, and be baptized
every one of you in the name of Jesus Christ for the
remission of sins, and ye shall receive the gift of the Holy
Ghost. For the promise is unto you, and to your children,
and to all that are afar off, even as many as the LORD
our God shall call.*

Acts 2:38,39

*But when they believed Philip preaching the things con-
cerning the kingdom of God, and the name of Jesus Christ,
they were baptized, both men and women. Now when
the apostles which were at Jerusalem heard that Samaria
had received the word of God, they sent unto them Peter
and John: Who, when they were come down, prayed for
them, that they might receive the Holy Ghost: (For as yet
he was fallen upon none of them: only they were baptized
in the name of the Lord Jesus.) Then laid they their hands
on them, and they received the Holy Ghost.*

Acts 8:12,14-17

*And Ananias went his way, and entered into the house;
and putting his hands on him said, Brother Saul, the
Lord, even Jesus, that appeared unto thee in the way as*

*thou camest, hath sent me, that thou mightest receive thy
sight, and be filled with the Holy Ghost.*

Acts 9:17

*And it came to pass, that, while Apollos was at Corinth,
Paul having passed through the upper coasts came
to Ephesus: and finding certain disciples, He said
unto them, Have ye received the Holy Ghost since ye
believed? And they said unto him, We have not so much
as heard whether there be any Holy Ghost. And he said
unto them, Unto what then were ye baptized? And they
said, Unto John's baptism. And when Paul had laid his
hands upon them, the Holy Ghost came on them; and
they spake with tongues, and prophesied.*

Acts 19:1-3,6

*While Peter yet spake these words, the Holy Ghost fell on
all them which heard the word. And they of the circum-
cision which believed were astonished, as many as came
with Peter, because that on the Gentiles also was poured
out the gift of the Holy Ghost. For they heard them speak
with tongues, and magnify God.*

Acts 10:44-46

*For he that speaketh in an unknown tongue speaketh
not unto men, but unto God: for no man understandeth
him; howbeit in the spirit he speaketh mysteries. I thank
my God, I speak with tongues more than ye all.*

1 Corinthians 14:2,18

In the last day, that great day of the feast, Jesus stood and cried, saying, If any man thirst, let him come unto me, and drink. He that believeth on me, as the scripture hath said, out of his belly shall flow rivers of living water. (But this spake he of the Spirit, which they that believe on him should receive: for the Holy Ghost was not yet given; because that Jesus was not yet glorified.)

John 7:37–39

If a son shall ask bread of any of you that is a father, will he give him a stone? or if he ask a fish, will he for a fish give him a serpent? Or if he shall ask an egg, will he offer him a scorpion? If ye then, being evil, know how to give good gifts unto your children: how much more shall your heavenly Father give the Holy Spirit to them that ask him?

Luke 11:11–13

Jesus said, *And, behold, I send the promise of my Father upon you: but tarry ye in the city of Jerusalem, until ye be endued with power from on high.*

Luke 24:49

But ye shall receive power, after that the Holy Ghost is come upon you: and ye shall be witnesses unto me both in Jerusalem, and in all Judaea, and in Samaria, and unto the uttermost part of the earth.

Acts 1:8

Books by Norvel Hayes

Don't Let the Devil Steal Your Destiny
How to Live and Not Die
Worship
The Blessing of Obedience
The Chosen Fast
Confession Brings Possession
How To Get Your Prayers Answered
Let Not Your Heart Be Troubled
Misguided Faith
The Number One Way To Fight the Devil
What To Do for Healing

Available from your local bookstore.

HARRISON HOUSE
P.O. Box 35035
Tulsa, OK 74153

About the Author

Norvel Hayes is a successful business-man, internationally renowned Bible teacher, and founder of several Christian ministries in the U.S. and abroad.

Brother Hayes founded *New Life Bible College*, located in Cleveland, Tennessee, in 1977. *New Life Bible Church* grew out of the Bible school's chapel services. The Bible School offers a two-year diploma and off-campus correspondence courses. Among its many other out-reaches, the church ministers God's Word and hot meals daily to the poor through the *New Life Soup Kitchen.*

Brother Hayes is also the founder and president of *New Life Maternity Home,* a ministry dedicated to the spiritual, physical and financial needs of young girls during pregnancy; *Campus Challenge,* an evangelistic outreach that distributes Christian literature on college campuses across America; *Street Reach,* a ministry dedicated to runaway teens located in Daytona Beach, Florida; and *Children's Home,* an orphanage home and education center located in India.

Known internationally for his dynamic exposition of the Word of God, Brother Hayes spends most of his time teaching and ministering God's deliverance and healing power in churches, college classrooms, conventions, and seminars around the world.

For a complete list of tapes and books by
Norvel Hayes, write:

Norvel Hayes
P.O. Box 1379
Cleveland, TN 37311

PRAYER OF SALVATION

God loves you—no matter who you are, no matter what your past. God loves you so much that He gave His one and only begotten Son for you. The Bible tells us that "...whoever believes in Him shall not perish but have eternal life" (John 3:16 NIV). Jesus laid down His life and rose again so that we could spend eternity with Him in heaven and experience His absolute best on earth. If you would like to receive Jesus into your life, say the following prayer out loud and mean it from your heart.

Heavenly Father, I come to You admitting that I am a sinner. Right now, I choose to turn away from sin, and I ask You to cleanse me of all unrighteousness. I believe that Your Son, Jesus, died on the cross to take away my sins. I also believe that He rose again from the dead so that I might be forgiven of my sins and made righteous through faith in Him. I call upon the name of Jesus Christ to be the Savior and Lord of my life. Jesus, I choose to follow You and ask that You fill me with the power of the Holy Spirit. I declare that right now I am a child of God. I am free from sin and full of the righteousness of God. I am saved in Jesus' name. Amen.

If you prayed this prayer to receive Jesus Christ as your Savior for the first time, please contact us on the Web at **www.harrisonhouse.com** to receive a free book.

Or you may write to us at

Harrison House • P.O. Box 35035 • Tulsa, Oklahoma 74153